THE
THREE MASKS
OF
AMERICAN
TRAGEDY

D0713407

THE
THREE MASKS
OF
AMERICAN
TRAGEDY

DAN VOGEL

LOUISIANA STATE UNIVERSITY PRESS / BATON ROUGE

ISBN 0-8071-0066-8
Library of Congress Catalog Card Number 73-90865
Copyright © 1974 by Louisiana State University Press
All rights reserved
Manufactured in the United States of America
Printed by The TJM Corporation, Baton Rouge, Louisiana
Designed by Albert R. Crochet

To my wife Sybil
More precious than pearls

Contents

Introduction

Literature is replete with studies of tragedy. Philosophers, critics, and playwrights themselves have all contributed. It's a long time and a lengthy bibliography from Aristotle's *Poetics* to Arthur Miller's "Tragedy and the Common Man" (1949). These two essays not only form a kind of parentheses in point of time, they also engender, through the title of Miller's essay, the first important question that must be faced in a study of American tragedy: can there be a tragedy of the common man?

Long-range critiques of this noble genre—say, Oscar Mandel's *A Definition of Tragedy* (1961), Elder Olson's *Tragedy and the Theory of Drama* (1961), and Cleanth Brooks's collection of essays, *Tragic Themes in Western Literature* (1955)—all ignore or quickly dispose of "American tragedy." Only Herbert Muller in *The Spirit of Tragedy* (1956) and Richard Sewall in *The Vision of Tragedy* (1959) show some respect. Sewall, in fact, devotes three chapters to individual works of tragedy in American literature, all novels. Regarding twentieth-century tragic drama, the attack has been even more ferocious. Joseph Wood Krutch in "The Tragic Fallacy," a 1929 essay stalwart enough to be reprinted in a book in 1956 without change, argued so strenuously that a realistic world cannot produce a vision properly called tragic, that John Gassner was intimidated into labeling the tragedies of past halcyon days as "high tragedy" and our meager contributions as "low tragedy." [1]

On the other hand, enough critics have written enough essays referring to tragic elements in the works discussed in this study to warrant the assumption that they are tragedies. More significantly, the authors themselves thought they were writing tragedies. Theirs was not a biased or intuitive claim. In essays, letters, and other statements, some of our tragic novelists and playwrights ruminate on the traditions of tragedy and how they fit into them. There is no call to "prove" their works as tragedies, and the purpose of this book is not to "test" them as such.

The scrutiny that these plays and novels have undergone regarding their tragic qualities has heretofore been individual and piecemeal. There is no study, to my knowledge, that has attempted to view American tragic writing as a cohesive genre, to discover overall concepts of tragedy in our democratic literature, and to point out lines of continuity in theme and method. This book is such an effort.

Tragedy in America is only a bit more than a century old, a pittance of time. But already we see that the world of our first tragedians, Hawthorne and Melville, was a different world. Their era was both religious and romantic, permitting a flamboyance of plot, character, speech, and symbol that is unfashionable in the realistic environment of this century. What they only anticipated and passed on to their literary progeny—the impersonal world of technology, the disoriented world of the subconscious, the alienated world of religious apostasy—has become the actual ambience of the twentieth century. The hero has become

---

1. Joseph Wood Krutch, "The Tragic Fallacy," *The Modern Temper* (New York: Harcourt, Brace, 1956); John Gassner, "Tragic Perspectives: A Series of Queries," in John D. Hurrell (ed.), *Two Modern American Tragedies* (New York: Scribner's, 1961), 26.

a narrower person; his dialogue approaches inability to articulate; the challenges he faces have been contracted into commonplace problems. There is little wonder that Krutch could not see tragedy arising from such an ignoble world where only surrogates for a deity display their power and small-time heroes confront them.

Thus, the major critical storm about American tragedy has erupted around the twentieth-century attempt to make society a force powerful enough to instigate a tragic enactment and sustain a tragic mood. Since society is presumably a mere man-made institution, the doubt seems well taken. For what man creates, man can improve, thus eliminating society as a tragic force. "Tragedy in the classic sense," avers Krutch, "insists that the universe rather than society is the ultimate cause of the human predicament." [2] More leniently, Herbert Muller refrains from excommunicating such works, but does see dramas of "social and political injustice" that ask for social action as "impure art":

> A writer treating [such] timely theme[s] will not achieve the full tragic effect unless he brings out its timeless implications [such as] a sense that the injustice is not merely the fault of a particular society, but the age-old story of man's inhumanity to man; that we can never do everything about it that we might like to do, or ought to do; that at best there will always remain suffering beyond remedy, bringing us back to the painful mystery of man's being in a mysterious universe.[3]

Yet Lionel Trilling sees possibilities of tragedy in stories about society:

> It would seem that a true knowledge of society comprehends the reality of the social forces it presumes to study and is aware of contradictions and consequences; it knows that

2. Joseph Wood Krutch, "Why O'Neill's Star Is Rising," *New York Times Magazine*, March 19, 1961, p. 108.
3. Herbert J. Muller, *The Spirit of Tragedy* (1956; reprint, New York: Washington Square Press, 1965), 13.

> sometimes society offers an opposition of motives in which
> the antagonists are in such a balance of authority and appeal
> that a man who so wholly perceives them as to embody them
> in his very being cannot choose between them and is therefore
> destroyed. This is known as tragedy.[4]

This, American tragedy, especially of our century, has sought to depict.

Perhaps I am leaving too apologetic an impression. The "small-fry" tragic heroes of American literature have nothing to be ashamed of. In their chromosomes they carry the genealogy of heroes of magnitude who are part of Western culture. The masks of American tragic heroes are those of Oedipus Tyrannos, Christ, and Satan. That's no mean ancestry.

Of these, the most prominent type of tragic hero is the tyrannos. Perhaps, since tragedy is a literary genre, the figure of Oedipus, the great Greek tyrannos and Aristotle's chief exemplar in the *Poetics*, loomed largest in the minds of American tragedians. But he did so because of a growing doubt in the hallowed myths of America which were based on know-how, self-reliance, and pragmatic success. Writers afflicted with this new tragic vision turned to find in Sophocles' drama the literary archetype of the conflict and affirmation they sought. Of the thirteen works I consider, eight fall into this category.

Oedipus, however, is not the whole configuration of American tragedy, by any means. American tragedians grow up in a Christian world. From this tradition come the tragic Christs and Satans who are the protagonists of several of our greatest tragedies. Though fewer in number than the tyrannoi, these grandiose protagonists, too, will receive the

4. Lionel Trilling, "The Princess Cassamassima," *The Liberal Imagination: Essays on Literature and Society* (1950; reprint, Garden City, N.Y.: Doubleday, 1953), 85.

attention due them. We shall find no medieval languishing Jesuses or simplistic unidimensional Satans, but vigorous figures of irony and tragedy. The truth is that the lineaments of one type of tragic hero are merged into another. Thus the reader is called upon to note, for example, that the moral predestination that underscores the tragedy of Christ inspirits the tragedy of a tyrannos like Willie Stark, of a demonic hero like Joe Christmas, as well as of a nearly divine innocent like Santiago, the old fisherman. And conversely, the satanism of an Ahab can be seen in a tyrannos like Thomas Sutpen and perhaps perceived even in Billy Budd, who, after all, killed a man. But the best method of presenting them is to emphasize the tradition and the dominant features of each type separately. This procedure, hopefully, will cut not only through each mask (to paraphrase a metaphor from *Moby-Dick*), but will reveal reasons why American tragedians etched into each mask resemblances of the others.

Not all American tragedies are noticed here. I have ignored what were billed as tragedies prior to Nathaniel Hawthorne's *Scarlet Letter* in 1850 as not truly representative of the genre in America. Models after Dryden or Tate, though written here, will teach us little. Nor do I treat Henry James's *Portrait of a Lady*, F. Scott Fitzgerald's *Great Gatsby*, and T. S. Eliot's *Family Reunion* and *Murder in the Cathedral*. Interpreting the first three would mean belaboring points I make elsewhere. The last is obviously and admittedly patterned on the medieval saint's play; my words would be tangential.

Nonetheless, the bag is mixed and representative. Here are nineteenth- and twentieth-century tragedies; tragedies of New England, New York, and the South; neopagan and neo-Christian; Greek and Hebraic; heroes and heroines; grandiose figures and schnooks. American tragedy is truly various, but there are cohesive threads that make it recognizably American. Like Tom Sawyer and Becky Thatcher, we shall follow the threads to where the light of understanding glows. I like that allusion for it gives me the opportunity to admit that the cave is dark and deep, and this will be an exploration that can only be incomplete. Yet explore we shall.

All the defects herein are mine. Whatever is valuable has been helped to become so by my colleagues at Stern College for Women, Yeshiva University: Dr. Morris Epstein, Dr. Carol Silver, Dr. Doris Shores, and Mrs. Laurel Hatvary; and by Dr. George Hatvary of St. John's University in New York. For creating legible typescripts of various versions of the manuscript from crabbed handwriting, I thank Miss Debby Ramras and Mrs. Bernice Linder. To Mrs. Marie Carmichael, who edited the typescript at the Louisiana State University Press, my deepest appreciation for her skill, care, and interest. My appreciation goes also to the staffs of the libraries at the Hebrew University in Jerusalem and at Stern College. To my children, Simeon, Mindy, and Jeremy, I am grateful for their patience. To my wife, my gratitude is nigh ineffable.

Dan Vogel

Brooklyn, N.Y.
May, 1973

THE
THREE MASKS
OF
AMERICAN
TRAGEDY

Prolegomenon:

The Shadow of Aristotle

"Aristotle seems to be in vogue," complained Richard Watts, drama critic of the New York *Post,* in 1961. "A number of pundits have been complaining that modern tragedy refuses to adhere to the rules he had laid down, and I can't see why it should be confined by them. . . . The insistence strikes me as pedantic and culturally snobbish." [1]

Nevertheless, Aristotle has given us a term of literary criticism, with a stated definition and set of characteristics, that has become a coin of communication among students of literature. If today one ignores his definition or redefines the term too freely, then he is guilty of destroying it as an intermediary among scholars. So we are faced with the meaning of the term "tragedy" in the context of American literature. This, of course, requires a review of the *Poetics,* for the *Poetics* and classical tragedy formed an influence upon American tragic writers. Practicing tragedians, like Herman Melville, Eugene O'Neill, Arthur Miller, Tennessee Williams, Maxwell Anderson, acknowledged (directly or indirectly) Aristotle's hovering presence. They were well aware of the definition of tragedy that over the ensuing two thousand years delimited the form into certain *sine qua non:* (1) "Tragedy, then, is an imitation of an action that is serious, complete and of a certain magnitude; in language embellished with each kind of artistic ornament,

1. New York *Post,* December 19, 1961.

3

the several kinds being found in separate parts of the play; in the form of action, not of narrative; through pity and fear effecting the proper purgation of these emotions [catharsis]" (Chapter 6).[2] (2) The plot should be complex, that is, one including "Reversal of the Situation . . . a change by which the action veers around to its opposite [peripety]. . . . Recognition . . . a change from ignorance to knowledge [anagnorisis]. . . . The Scene of Suffering . . . a destructive or painful action . . ." (Chapter 11). (3) The hero should be "a man who is not eminently good and just, yet whose misfortune is brought about not by vice or depravity, but by some error or frailty [*hamartia*]. He must be one who is highly renowned and prosperous, a personage like Oedipus, Thyestes, or other such illustrious men of such families" (Chapter 13).

The challenge of American tragedians was to absorb, sift, and fulfill the residual qualities of tragedy to fit the society and time for which they were writing. The first revision is quite clear. New literary forms emended Aristotle's expectation that the drama, not other styles of narrative, was the only proper form of tragedy. By the time Hawthorne wrote *The Scarlet Letter*, the novel had reached such a status that its form could be included in the holy canon of tragedy. But perhaps Aristotle, even here, was more right than I have credited him: academic critics love to break up novels into dramatic cycles.

In other aspects, the evolution of Aristotle's requisites is more subtle. That a tragic hero is necessary is undoubted, but the status of the hero, the terms of his tragedy, and the nature of his heroism have changed. That peripety is a necessary component of plot is clear, but the nature of peripety

2. S. H. Butcher (trans.), *Aristotle's Poetics* (New York: Hill and Wang, 1961). To accommodate readers with other editions of the treatise, I shall cite only the chapters, since they are very brief anyway.

had to be changed for a democratic literature. That anag-norisis is a climax differentiating tragedy from other forms of plot remains a principle, but the nature of it and the effect of it have been revised. Finally, catharsis is perhaps the one trait of tragedy that has remained unchanged since Aristotle passingly defined it.

Over all, as we shall see when we come to consider in-dividual works, the specter of magnitude looms. Can a hero arising from the *demos*, with his limited commonplace problems, without the aura of royalty and the mystique of noble family, be involved in an imitation of an action leading to catharsis? On this point, Joseph Wood Krutch, in "The Tragic Fallacy," condemned Ibsen's *Ghosts* and, through it, all modern tragedy (except O'Neill's). Yet American tragic writers seemed to face up to the matter.

Let us examine each of Aristotle's essential aspects more closely in the frame of reference of American tragedy. To judge from the *Poetics*, catharsis is the central concept. In-deed, "Aristotle came very close to a definition of what tragedy is in his famous passage on catharsis," wrote Max-well Anderson.[3] Though there has been little agreement throughout the ages about the precise meaning of the term, on one tenet there has been basic agreement: catharsis has something to do with the audience response to the tragedy. All other literary forms are defined by their inner charac-teristics and structure. An epic or a sonnet, for example, is so called by virtue of length, technique, structure, rhyme scheme, and similar objective conventions. It remains an entry in its genre if no one but its author was affected by it. By Aristotle's definition of tragedy, however, there must be an audience response that he called catharsis; if not, the work is not a tragedy.

3. Maxwell Anderson, *The Essence of Tragedy and Other Footnotes and Papers* (1939; reprint, New York: Russell and Russell, 1970), 3.

In truth, this is as much a problem for the critic as for the author. Eric Bentley, writing about *Death of a Salesman*, asserted, "When Willy falls never to rise again, we go home feeling purged of (or by) pity and terror." [4] How does Bentley know how we feel? Is tragedy to be judged by a majority vote of an audience? Or is Bentley judging from his own response? Most likely the latter is true. Yet on this subjective basis tragedies must be judged and are judged. The authors know it, and when inspired by their tragic vision to formulate a tragedy, they strike beyond their normal aspirations of trying to write a play or novel that will be liked. They try to arouse those specific emotions—pity and terror—that Aristotle identified. This is, indeed, Tennessee Williams' justification for the kind of plays he writes: "If there is any truth in the Aristotelian idea that violence is purged by its poetic representation on a stage, then it may be that my cycle of violent plays have had a moral justification after all.... I have always felt a release from the sense of meaninglessness and death when a work of tragic intention has seemed to me to have achieved that intention, even if only approximately, nearly." [5]

Yet, Aristotle's catharsis is still one of the most troublesome terms in literary criticism. For two millennia, his concept of purgation through pity and terror proved obscure. Finally, with laudable pride, Stephen Dedalus, in James Joyce's *A Portrait of the Artist as a Young Man*, helped settle the matter: "Pity is the feeling which arrests the mind in the presence of whatsoever is grave and constant in human sufferings and unites it with the human sufferer. Terror is the feeling which arrests the mind in the presence of

4. Eric Bentley, "Better than Europe?" in John D. Hurrell (ed.), *Two Modern American Tragedies* (New York: Scribner's, 1961), 132.
5. New York *Times*, March 8, 1959, Sec. 2, p. 1.

whatsoever is grave and constant in human sufferings and unites it with the secret cause." [6]

Roy Morrell has offered a psychoanalytic explanation of why the audience participates in catharsis and why the process is pleasurable. First, it strengthens the psyche "by means of shocks from the outside . . . mild, preventive, re-organizing ones." Secondly, an empathy with the hero is created because this hero is true to life and faces up to his responsibilities, and thereby stands in for us in the suffering of these shocks. The enactment of the tragic process helps the audience "to experience in his fantasy something which has been evaded in the past." Catharsis, then, is being forced to face almost directly and personally the terror of the hero and thereby to reach the peace of self-revelation. [7] To achieve these results, American tragedians had to re-define Aristotle's other tenets of tragedy.

Plot, Aristotle insists, "should imitate actions which excite pity and fear, this being the distinctive mark of tragic imitation" (Chapter 13). But, in order to excite pity and fear, our tragic writers no longer believe, as Aristotle did, that "plot . . . is the first principle, and, as it were, the soul of a tragedy: Character holds the second place" (Chapter 6). Rather, in our literature, especially in the twentieth century, the reverse is true. The magnitude of tragic plot is no longer measured by the magnitude of action. The criterion is depth of character. The burden of achieving catharsis in tragedy in democratic literature has shifted to the hero, who carries the mystique of the Individual. Today, character is primary; the actions often are small and narrow.

6. James Joyce, *A Portrait of the Artist as a Young Man* (1916; reprint, New York: Signet, 1954), 159.

7. Roy Morrell, "The Psychology of Tragic Pleasure," in Laurence Michel and Richard Sewall (eds.), *Tragedy: Modern Essays in Criticism* (Englewood Cliffs, N.J.: Prentice-Hall, 1963), 286.

It seems to me, however, that Aristotle anticipated this shift of emphasis that American tragedians have capitalized on. In his discussion of tragic plot, Aristotle designates peripety as an essential distinguishing element. The change of fortune, he points out, from Oedipus' high estate as king of Thebes to the disaster of pollution, blindness, and exile is the paramount plot characteristic of the play. But the series of incidents, by itself, is not enough. Aristotle demands, in addition, probability in the sequence of incidents that form the peripety (Chapter 7). This leads Francis Fergusson to point out, "*Action* (praxis) does not mean deeds, events, or physical activity: it means, rather, the motivation from which deeds spring." [8] Motivation is the essence of probability; it lies in the character, not the actions, of the tragic hero.

Obviously the device of political rank is the most direct symbol of noble character as far as Aristotle, Shakespeare, Corneille, and Racine were concerned. The validity of their view cannot be denied even today. Audiences still flock unquestioningly and will respond unstintingly to classical and Elizabethan tragedies about individuals who deal with problems long dead and foreign—like the staying of a plague at Thebes or a curse upon the ancient house of Atreus or the succession to the throne of Denmark. Democratic audiences naturally cut through the external trapping of nobility of older heroes to recognize their human nature, and they become heroic because of that, not because of coronets or epaulets. Beside them strides the universal little man who is also heroic and tragic, destined in American tragedy to become the typical tragic hero. Being born into the accursed house of Laius, like Oedipus, or into the accursed

8. Francis Fergusson, introduction to S. H. Butcher (trans.), *Aristotle's Poetics* (New York: Hill and Wang, 1961), 8.

house of Atreus, like Orestes, is not too far different from being born into an accursed society, like Joe Christmas in the South or Mio Romagna in the North.

Social evolution has redefined nobility as not of the blood but of the spirit, since virtue, as Aristotle saw, remains a necessary characteristic of a tragic hero. But there is some difficulty even here that may be exemplified by two statements that Oscar Mandel makes in *A Definition of Tragedy*. At one point Mandel declares that "goodness in a protagonist is an absolute requisite of tragedy." But later he writes that a hero cannot be other than one who "commands our good will ... [and] command[s] sufficient approval" to cause an audience to deplore his suffering.[9] These, however, are not identical requisites; they may even be oppositional. The new criminology, based upon liberal Christianity and sociology, has convinced us that there are no villains in today's society, only victims of the subconscious or of the environment. Their vice and depravity may easily be clothed with latent and dormant virtue. Their reaction to the heredity and environment that formed them may very well be a factor in their heroism. Aristotle's hero must be reinterpreted by reference only to Mandel's second point: the tragic protagonist must engender our goodwill.

Such a concept of heroism demands a concomitant shift from action to character in the peripety as well. True, conventional peripety is visible in the careers of American tragic heroes like Captain Ahab, Willie Stark, and Thomas Sutpen. But how much further down can Joe Christmas, Willy Loman, and Blanche DuBois go? The peripety of the latter three must be described wholly in terms of their hu-

9. Oscar Mandel, *A Definition of Tragedy* (New York: New York University Press, 1961), 89, 138.

man spirit, as a process of dehumanization by outside forces. If that process were completed, then we would have some kind of melodrama, but the idea of tragedy calls for the arrest of those forces somewhere near the denouement and a balancing by the resuscitated heroism of the protagonist. The suspicions of greatness that lay latent in the common-born hero now emerge forcefully; he becomes worthy of equilibrating unstoppable powers, and catharsis is aroused.

The last gasp of his heroism is aided by the two other aspects of tragic plot that Aristotle identified—anagnorisis and suffering. Anagnorisis has remained a *sine qua non* of the drama and, of course, of tragedy. If anything, it has taken on more importance. Indeed, Maxwell Anderson calls it "the mainstream in the mechanism of a modern play. . . . A play should lead up to and away from a central crisis; and this crisis should consist in a discovery by the leading character which has an indelible effect on his thought and emotion and completely alters his course of action." [10]

But "the recognition scene, as Aristotle isolated it in the tragedies of the Greeks, was generally an artificial device, a central scene in which the leading character saw through a disguise, recognized as a friend or as an enemy, perhaps as a lover," [11] and the like. As a mere device of spectacle, its usefulness is long past, for like other Aristotelian plot devices, it too has been shifted from a characteristic of the development of plot to a point in the evolution of character.

The area of discovery is no longer in the action of the play, but in the subtle milieu of the mind of the hero where we are expected to witness the change from ignorance to knowledge. As Anderson says: "For the mainspring in the mechanism of a modern play it is almost invariably a discovery of the hero of some element in his environment or in

---

10. Anderson, *The Essence of Tragedy*, 6.   11. *Ibid.*, 5.

his own soul of which he has not been aware—or which he has not taken sufficiently into account." Anagnorisis is an invariable characteristic of modern tragedy, but has been changed. It has become enriched and sophisticated, for now, in Anderson's concluding words: "The essence of tragedy . . . is the spiritual awakening, or regeneration, of his hero." [12]

For Aristotle, suffering, like anagnorisis, is but mere spectacle, a single episode, almost an appendage on the plot. These two sentences are his entire statement on the subject: "The third part [of the plot] is the Scene of Suffering. The Scene of Suffering is a destructive or painful action, such as death on the stage, bodily agony, wound and the like" (Chapter 11). Here, again, an element of plot was shifted to an element of character. The American hero is, as we shall see, a Christian tyrannos, and a Christian tyrannos suffers. It is his Christological heritage. For American tragedians, suffering is the simultaneous, protracted, omnipresent burden of the hero, from almost the beginning to his definite end. There is no American tragic hero who is free from pain when the story opens, and it is the pain which contributes to the anagnorisis that climaxes his tragedy.

Thus, it is with obeisance to the universal essentials of the *Poetics* that modern tragic writers acknowledge the influence of Aristotle. It is with independent insight into the needs, fears, and aspirations of their democratic society that they have revised what he had written. His are the major avenues to catharsis; their job is to provide the contemporaneously proper vehicles. What is perhaps ironic is that the ancient critic would have treated their attempts more kindly than do his modern progeny among critics. After all, he himself said of Euripides: "The best proof is that, on the

---

12. *Ibid.*, 10.

stage and in dramatic competition such plays [like Euripides'], if well worked out, are the most tragic in effect; and
Euripides, faulty though he may be in the general manage-
ment of his subject, yet is felt to be the most tragic of the
poets" (Chapter 13).

Faulty as our tragic writers may be, they ought not to be
denied their place as tragic poets in the long and honored
history of the genre. Aristotle would have been their first
sponsor.

I

sa

The Mask of Oedipus Tyrannos

BY WAY OF DEFINITION

One of the singular features in the history of tragedy is the fact that this genre of literature flourishes at a time of prosperity for the respective societies in which it was written. Thus Greek tragedy came at the precise moment of the golden age of Athens, when her power and politics were preeminent. Elizabethan and French tragedy came at a time of those nations' high achievement. In America, tragedy was first written in the middle of the nineteenth century, coincident with the supreme confidence of a republic flexing its manifest destiny. Perhaps the fearful concepts that underlie tragedy can be faced only at times of high human power; perhaps tragedy is the instinctive literary corrective during these moments of cocky pride.

Of all these societies, America's was the most boyishly optimistic. When its first two tragedies were published, it had no history of tragic wars from which to cull tragic situations—only three successful campaigns of luck and persistence. It could look back upon two and a half centuries of unblemished success from the moment the first Briton set foot on what was to become Virginia, and it held a perfect faith of centuries to come of more of the same. It had few heroes, tragic or otherwise.

And yet America was born with a sense of tragedy. Puritan Massachusetts was based on a dogma of natural evil. A sense of natural evil was present among even the halcyon generation following the Revolution, when Charles Brockden Brown and Edgar Allan Poe thrilled America with stories of death, darkness, and mystery. Beneath the absurd Gothic exterior and grotesquerie, their novels and stories revealed a real feeling of pervasive, inexplicable evil that comes unbeknownst and uncontrolled from both within and without mankind. They anticipated the introduction of tragedy into the literature of a buoyant, democratic society.

American tragic writing normally has its social and historical roots in the three provisions of what the eminent historian of the American intellect, Ralph Henry Gabriel, called the "fundamental law" of American democracy: the existence and operation of universal morality; the sanctity of the individual and individualism; the goodness and inevitability of progress.[1] These basic tenets of American thought, together with their corollaries and contradictions, provide insights into the American character from which arises the concept of the most important type of American tragic hero—the tyrannos.

The etymologists point out that the word *tyrannos* in original usage was not pejorative. It had once meant "kingly, lordly, in a good sense," according to W. W. Skeat, "as in the tragedians." [2] H. W. Fowler adds, "The word connoted the manner in which it was exercised; despotic or 'tyrannical' use of the usurped position was natural and common, but incidental only." [3] Writing about Sophocles' famous hero, Bernard Knox insists upon calling him "Oedi-

1. Ralph Henry Gabriel, *The Course of American Democratic Thought* (2nd ed.; New York: Ronald, 1956), 14–15.
2. W. W. Skeat, *An Etymological Dictionary of the English Language* (London: Clarendon, 1968), 676–77.
3. H. W. Fowler, *A Dictionary of Modern English Usage*, ed. Ernest Gowers (2nd ed.; London: Oxford, 1965), 656.

pus tyrannos." We shall later consider the literary legacy of this drama; here we are interested in Knox's definition of the term:

> The word tyrannos has a larger significance [than is evident in the narrative incidents of the play]. Oedipus . . . is a paradigm, an example to all men; and the fact that he is a tyrannos, self-made ruler, the proverbial Greek example of worldly success won by individual intelligence and exertion, makes him an appropriate symbol of civilized man, who was beginning to believe, in the 5th century B.C., that he could seize control of his own destiny . . . through knowledge, ingenuity, and technique.[4]

These qualities and the fate of Oedipus characterize not only the hero of tragedy in the fifth century B.C. in Greece; they characterize the hero of tragedy in the nineteenth and twentieth centuries in America. For the tyrannos of America carried his ancient lineage into a land that was not under an aristocracy, but proudly democratic; not at the apogee of its history, but preening itself as a new Eden; not subject to pagan gods, but answerable to one universal, moral Deity.

DARKNESS IN EDEN

Our belief in universal morality was derived from two sources: the natural order and Christianity. The effect of dogmatic Christianity on American tragic writing will be discussed later. Here we shall center our attention on the promises of nature in the Eden called America.

The intellectual heritage of America taught that nature was good. The observation of nature (as well as Christian belief) provided evidence that the order of the cosmos was regulated by harmony, the origin of which was an intelli-

4. Bernard Knox, "Sophocles' Oedipus," in Cleanth Brooks (ed.), *Tragic Themes in Western Literature* (1955; reprint, New Haven: Yale University Press, 1960), 5, 9.

gent, beneficent First Cause. This was the teaching of the Bible, and of Plato and the Greeks; this was the implication of the most important formulation of natural laws (prior to Charles Darwin's) in intellectual history—those of Isaac Newton.[5] This article of faith permeated the writings of America's favorite British authors—John Milton, William Wordsworth, Samuel Taylor Coleridge, Thomas Carlyle. The aspect of virgin nature on this continent drove Cotton Mather in 1702 into a paroxysm of prophetic optimism: " 'Tis possible that our Lord Jesus Christ carried thousands of *Reformers* into the retirements of an *American Desert*, on purpose, that, withe an opportunity granted unto many of his Faithful Servants, to enjoy the precious *Liberty* of their ministry." [6] In the next 120 years, the American desert became a veritable Eden.

The sense of harmony and the sense of place, the structure of coordination and inevitability were considered to be merely the physical manifestations of the providence that permeates creation. Nature is the reflection of the good; in and through nature, therefore, the good can be intuited. Developing a new natural Christianity for the new nation, Ralph Waldo Emerson in 1836 expressed the dogma in an essay called "Nature": "What is a farm but a mute gospel? The chaff and the wheat, weeds and plants, blight, rain, insects, sun—it is a sacred emblem from the first furrow of spring to the last stack which the snow of winter overtakes in the field. . . . Nor can it be doubted that this moral sentiment which thus scents the air, grows in the grain, and impregnates the waters of the world, is caught by man and sinks into his soul." [7]

5. Gabriel, *American Democratic Thought*, 14–15.

6. Cotton Mather, "Magnalia Christi Americana," in R. H. Pearce (ed.), *Colonial American Writing* (New York: Rinehart, 1961), 138–39.

7. Stephen E. Whicher (ed.), *Selections from Ralph Waldo Emerson* (Boston: Houghton, Mifflin, 1967), 39.

In England, nature was looked upon in two ways—pantheistically, as a force in its own right, to be valued and almost worshiped, as by a Wordsworth or a Coleridge or a Byron; or transcendentally, as a physical symbol of spirit, a far inferior and subserving spirit. These responses are, for most, worlds apart. As Leon Howard remarked, one cannot be a nature lover and a transcendentalist at the same time.[8] Yet Emerson reconciled the two nature-intoxicated views. He added the fillip of reality to transcendentalism, testing it by America's chief philosophical test—common experience. For him, the first inalienable right of man was a love of nature, through which the divine spark in man could be nourished.[9]

Earlier, Jefferson had seen in nature the authority for the natural political and social rights of man. Man was as much a part of harmonious nature as the relationship of pollen and wind. Newtonian laws of cosmic mechanics simply point the way to the laws of social mechanics. The rights of man are as natural and inevitable as the physical laws of nature. Therefore they are equally inalienable. The cadences in which Jefferson expressed these rights in the Declaration of Independence are justly famous, not only because of the incandescent moment of history in which they appeared, but because the doctrine of natural social philosophy inspirits the American character to this day.

In America, the argument of natural rights could not stand alone. We must remember that the fountainhead of America, Massachusetts, began as a Holy Christian (*i.e.,* Puritan) Commonwealth. Natural rights had to be seen also as religious sanctions endowed, as Jefferson said, by the Cre-

8. Leon Howard, "Americanization of European Heritage," in Margaret Denny and William H. Gilman (eds.), *The American Writer and the European Tradition* (Minneapolis: University of Minnesota Press, 1950), 80.

9. *Ibid.,* 81.

ator. Ironically, however, as much as natural Christianity, as preached by Jefferson and Emerson, sanctified the freedom inherent in natural rights, it inhibited it is well. Despite agreement between Newtonian science and religion on the existence and beneficence of God, the operation of these laws upon man inhibits him. Essentially, he is an outsider looking in upon nature; he has no power to tamper with it. The moral law that inspired Emerson and Jefferson into ecstasies about individual freedom can be seen as the very instrument that contracts his liberty. In nature is a secrecy and power that rules and makes man no more than a beggar recipient of its bounty or of its denials.

This Emerson himself came to realize. In 1838, in a lecture on "The Tragic" (published in 1844), he does identify "the bitterest tragic element" as "the belief in brute Fate and Destiny; the belief that the order of Nature and events is controlled by a law not adapted to man . . . and heedless whether it serves or crushes him." [10] Such a bare notion is worthy of pagans like the Greek tragedians, he implies. But with us, by means of "reason and faith . . . the tragic element is somewhat circumscribed." Tragedy, it appears, is but another test of optimism. By 1850, however, Emerson joined Hawthorne and Melville, in that *annus mirabilis*, in the search for the serenity that comes after tragic vision: "The world is saturated with deity and law. [Man] is content with just and unjust, with sots and fools, with triumph of folly and fraud. He can behold with serenity the yawning gulf between the ambition of man and his power of performance, between the demand and the supply of power, which makes the tragedy of all souls." [11] Even in Eden there falls

10. E. W. Emerson (ed.), *Complete Works of Ralph Waldo Emerson* (12 vols.; Boston: Houghton, Mifflin, 1904), XII, 407, 408.
11. *Ibid.*, IV, 183.

a darkness. The promises of nature to the tyrannos may be simply the harbingers of disillusionment.

Indeed, as the century wore on and burst after 1865 into modern times, Nature would be transmuted into Naturalism, and man would be seen once again by some as the Puritans saw him, a being condemned to limitation and corruption. Old-time doctrinal predeterminism becomes scientific determinism. Though American society refashioned the age-old confrontation of man and God, above it all, however, like the spirit of God hovering above turbulent matter at the moment of creation, the belief in universal morality still penetrates American life and the career of the hero caught in an *agon* between determinism and individualism. Though Eden was somewhat beclouded, the individual saw God as Providence, and he created a society in which he saw himself as a demigod.

THE MAKING OF THE AMERICAN TYRANNOS

The North American continent served to support a new individualistic society, one directed consciously not to restrictive class (as in Old England), or to a closed community (as in the Massachusetts Commonwealth), but to the free self-reliant individual. "The idea and reality of the open class system," declares Gabriel, "is perhaps the most important single contribution of Americans to the social thinking of Western civilization." [12]

Man, Thomas Jefferson believed, was basically good and inherently rational. Thus, when called upon to act, "if given freedom of choice, [each man] can be trusted to choose the wise and the good." [13] Jefferson's political faith was

12. Gabriel, *American Democratic Thought*, 16.
13. Paraphrased by Randall Stewart, *American Literature and Christian Doctrine* (Baton Rouge: Louisiana State University Press, 1958), 39–40.

echoed in the philosophical faith of Emerson. Emerson preaches in epigrams strewn throughout the essays prior to the 1850s that each individual has the ability to develop his own personality, indeed his own truths, through the agency of nature. Neither he, nor William James after him, feared what truths he would discover. Each man uniquely possesses both the spirit of God (soul) and His physical emanation (natural body). Therefore, man must be moral; therefore, his truths must be moral; therefore, he can—nay, he must—trust himself, as Emerson insisted. Thus evolved the most significant aspect of individualism—self-reliance.

The interaction of political philosophy and transcendentalism produced the new noble—the common man. All the ancient attributes of heroism—courage, leadership, ambition, nobility of spirit—become him. Thoreau's *Walden* describes on a small scale what the self-reliant man can do and be. The transmigration of the Alleghenies, usurpation of the Plains, and conquest of the Rockies by hordes of individuals are epic manifestations of the Concord sage's "practical idealism." Out of this experience came the "ideal of frontier society . . . the self-made man." [14] The frontier, as Frederick Jackson Turner emphasized, was the primary factor in forming the American character. But when that physical frontier disappeared, the concept of moral self-reliance did not disappear with it. Josiah Royce, noting the separation of individualism from its traditional place in nature, urged moral individualism to turn its attention to the community and to seek its freedom there.[15] Since this community, as we noted, was an open society, Royce's idea came to mean that the self-made-man-to-be saw society as an open, upward road. Upward mobility came to be the hall-

14. Richard Hofstadter, *The American Political Tradition* (New York: Vintage Books, 1948), 48.

15. Gabriel, *American Democratic Thought*, 308–309.

mark of the American character. The whole country took
on the lineaments of a tyrannos. And as the country fared,
so fared the individual tyrannos.

Richard Hofstadter gives two examples in political history that helped fashion the rags-to-riches myth or its vari-
ant, log-cabin-to-White-House. One of his exemplars is
Andrew Jackson, the first man to be elected from the back-
water and a piece of flint in the eye of the seaboard establish-
ment. Jackson represented, Hofstadter tells us, "the typical
American: the master mechanic who aspired to open his
own shop, the planter or farmer who speculated in land,
the lawyer who hoped to be a judge, the local politician
who wanted to go to Congress, the grocer who would be a
merchant." [16] These were, to Americans, noble aims, and
their achievement was ample evidence of the inherent nobility of the individual who achieved them. Every one of these
men is that hero of American individualistic possibility—
the common man with his shrewd eyes always upward.

In American mythology, Andrew Jackson is but a wraith
compared to the full-bodied mythic and epical figure that
Abraham Lincoln came to be. "He [Lincoln] became the
exemplar of the self-made man," asserts Hofstadter.[17] The
myth likes to relate stories of a gangling, pure, selfless saint.
But Hofstadter's portrait of Lincoln emphasizes the pragmatic forcefulness of his individualism. Lincoln was first
and exclusively a politician, that is, a manipulator of events
and of people, who had his eye always on the goal, and consciously bobbed and weaved, pushed and pulled to achieve
that goal. Circumstance and situation were merely the opportunity for, not the limitation of, his self-making. He applied shrewdness, candor, the carrot, and the stick as necessity demanded. There was nothing unvirtuous about this;

16. Hofstadter, *American Political Tradition*, 59.
17. *Ibid.*, 93, 94.

it was seen as entirely in keeping with the American character and tradition.[18]

But Lincoln has come to represent much more than this. He became a protagonist in "a drama in which a great man shoulders the torment and moral burdens of a blundering sinful people, suffers for them, and redeems them with hallowed Christian virtues—'malice toward none and charity for all'—and is destroyed at the pitch of his success." [19] Though Hofstadter wrote this passage as part of a political history, it contains all the characteristics of an American tragic hero.

To envision the common man as a self-reliant reflection of God is to do two things: first, to preserve the common man as a proper personality to have a relationship with an omnipotent Deity; secondly, to make self-reliance the *hamartia* that will lead him to tragic catastrophe. American tragic irony is born. In 1841, Emerson had written:

> We have yet had no genius in America, with tyrannous eye, which knew the value of our incomparable materials, and saw, in the barbarism and materialism of the times, another carnival of the same gods whose picture he so much admires in Homer; then in the Middle Ages; then in Calvinism. Banks and tariffs, the newspaper and caucus, Methodism and Unitarianism, are flat and dull to dull people, but rest on the same foundations of wonder as the town of Troy and the Temple of Delphi, and are as swiftly passing away.[20]

Ten years later came the response in the voice of Herman Melville in *Moby-Dick*: "If, then to meanest mariners, and renegades and castaways, I shall hereafter ascribe high qualities, though dark; [and] weave round them tragic graces . . . bear me out in it, thou great democratic God!" [21] The American tyrannos and God were on the same side.

18. *Ibid.*, 104–105, 117, 133–34, *passim.*   19. *Ibid.*, 93.
20. Whicher (ed.), *Selections from Emerson*, 238.
21. Herman Melville, *Moby-Dick, or the Whale*, ed. Luther Mansfield and

ONSLAUGHTS

In Melville's midcentury tragic novel, man was God's partner, for both manifest destiny and manifest tragedy. This exalted position, however, was about to be questioned. Since 1859, both man's position in the universe and the notion of inevitable and fruitful progress have been under reassessment. That date begins the crescendo of this revaluation for it is the year, of course, in which Darwin's *Origin of Species* was published. This is not the place to dwell lengthily on the history of Darwinism in American thought (see Richard Hofstadter's *Social Darwinism in American Thought*). But certain conclusions from the ensuing controversy may be mentioned.

Those who applied Darwinism pessimistically claimed that man was no longer a demigod in partnership with God; he became but a physical species caught up in a relentless natural evolution. The limitation of the individual's powers now became an irksome impotence in an impersonal relationship with impersonal locomotion. Newton's benign cosmic mechanics once was reflected in a vision of progressive social process; now Darwin's picture of rapacious nature reinterpreted self-reliance into an aristocracy of those who survived.

The evolution of American history presented empirical evidence of the rightness of this interpretation of Darwinism. The Civil War, the great fall from grace in the new Eden, marked the break in the manifest destiny of the nation. Old and new sins came to haunt America. The Great Fratricide certainly did not expiate the sin of slavery. And soon after, came the demise of the frontier, and the death of benign capitalism at the hands of rapacious industrialists

---

H. P. Vincent (Centenary ed.; New York: Hendricks House, 1952), Chap. 26, p. 114.

and financiers tolled the knell of the history of the self-reliant individual in the West. The survival of the fittest was an effective argument for the genocide of the American Indian. Finally, when in true Darwinian progress toward complexity, America started to become urban, urbanization became contaminated by uncontrolled technology. History became a curse that beset the present.

Social process, once the crowning characteristic of American progressivism, by the 1920s had come to pose a powerful threat to man's freedom. Society offered itself as the prevalent modern form of superhuman power, once the province of a personal God. The upward mobility of the common man was now suspected of merely aping the red-toothed process of survival. Success and survival became almost synonymous.

The new study of behaviorism similarly threatened traditional concepts of individualism and social progress. The mind, or spirit, of man and his community was once solely the concern of religion; now it became the concern of secular, objective interpreters of individual action and measures of communal tendencies. The predominant name here, of course, is Sigmund Freud. Freud's theories seemed to substantiate the power of uncontrollable process without progress. The world he described was fashioned before an individual's intelligence was mature enough to deal with it; and in addition, by that time he had the whole chaos of the subconscious to contend with. This again is a world the individual never made, against which he was expected to contend and attempt to control. The trouble is that this new cosmos is amoral, like Darwin's nature, and consequently perhaps more frightening and amorphous than God's old cosmos. Man's great evolutionary self-perpetuating bulwark against annihilation, his reason, now was devoted to explaining and controlling his own inner world of irrationality and unreason.

This is the black side of the picture; but not the least of America's great accomplishments, I think, is how this young republic marshaled its intellectual forces against these powerful onslaughts that seemed to declare her fundamental law quaint, naïve, and false. In each area of developing intellectual controversy—science, society, and psychology— arose champions of the old fundamental law who were able to argue in new terms of reference as well as in the old ones. There was John Wesley Powell in science, Lewis Morgan in sociology, and William James in psychology. All of them strove to reassert the sublimity of the individual.

Powell argued that the advancements of science were all due to discoveries by *individual* scientific thinkers. Progress in this apparently machinelike, cold, and impersonal intellectual pursuit is as dependent upon individual endeavor as any form of progress in the past. Using the very language of Darwinian naturalism, Morgan insisted that Darwin did not destroy the ideas of inevitable benign progress and self-reliance. Where Darwin preached a science of species in inexorable progression (not mere metamorphosis, Morgan insists), Morgan preached a science of individuals in the same inexorable progression.

Perhaps the most striking gathering of traditional forces in the face of the onslaught of new theories occurred in the area of interpreting the new psychology. William James formulated a synthesis of approach that neither ignored new scientific proofs of natural process nor discarded cherished dogmas of American thought. His "pragmatism" accepted the new view of the cosmos—fluxional, constantly contracting, expanding, decaying, and creating. He even followed the spoor of the idea that came to envision the machinations of God as finite. Nonetheless, when he came to formulate implications of the fluxional universe and the finity of God, he still was constrained to declare that God's existence is the guarantee of an ideal order that is eternal. Faith may no longer be a matter of dogma, but it is a matter of intuition, an intuition that places its bet on a progressive future.[22]

With the doctrine of intuition as strong in James as it was in his master Emerson, individualism remained as potent a concept in the new scientific philosophy of pragmatism as it was in moral transcendentalism. James's dogma—the creation of valid truths through the "radical empiricism" of the individual—had to depend upon the morality of the truth maker. Otherwise, all hell would break loose on man's earth. The individual had to be looked upon as a possessor of the will and the desire to transcend imperfection in the search for pragmatic truth. Clearly then, James's pragmatism is a restatement of the American fundamental law, this time in terms of scientific empiricism but retaining in it a moral God and moral men.

A good deal has happened in American life since Melville's creation of the gigantic sea captain as tragic hero. The undulation of God's relationship with the hero, the gap between promise and fulfillment, is still the subject of American tragedy, though the tyrannos is smaller and more inarticulate about his problems. What has happened has tended to cut down the size of the tragic hero, but it never touched his innate nobility and his ability to centralize our fears and make us proud and fearful of our aspirations. To help make him our dramatic alter ego, American tragedians called upon two ancient heroes—one, a commoner named Job; the other, a prince named Oedipus.

22. Gabriel, *American Democratic Thought*, on Powell, 180, 181; on Morgan, 176, 177; on James, 339, 345, 340.

THE SANCTIFICATION OF JOB

Though the word is Greek, the concept of the tyrannos is not exclusively so. The biblical figure Job was a type of tyrannos. That this kind of hero carries such a hallowed lineage within him is vital for a literature whose origins lie in Christian homiletics. The Book of Job has long been part of the fabric of American literature. Puritan elders sermonized upon it, and in the seventeenth century a multivolume work was published about it. Hawthorne's work two hundred years later reveals a deep and abiding interest in it;[23] and Melville's debt to the Book of Job in *Moby-Dick* alone requires five pages of notes in the Centenary edition of the novel.[24] Even in our apostate century, American authors have found the Book of Job fascinating. Thornton Wilder modernized the theme in a playlet, *Hast Thou Considered My Servant Job?* (1928). Thomas Wolfe, in an essay, called the book the "most tragic, sublime, and expression of human loneliness that I ever read," and its hero became for Wolfe "God's . . . tragic man." [25] Robert Frost unburdened his reactions to World War II symbolically in *A Masque of Reason* (1945), ending his use of Job-characters with the finis line, "Here endeth chapter forty-three of Job." For Archibald MacLeish, it served as the vehicle by which he could comment upon our generation's responses to God's modern displays of power (or malignity). His debt to his source is paid in the title of his play, *J. B.* (1958).

The Book of Job channels into American tragedy a number of concepts: the deterministic base of tragedy; the covenant of tragedy that ties God and man into inexorable roles;

---

23. Austin Warren, "Hawthorne's Reading," *New England Quarterly*, VIII (December, 1935), 494.
24. Melville, *Moby-Dick*, 699–703.
25. C. Hugh Holman (ed.), *The Thomas Wolfe Reader* (New York: Scribner's, 1962), 678–80, *passim*.

a teleology of pain; the irony that makes friends and lovers into antagonists; and finally, the supreme role that a common man can play in a tragic story.

For Job was a common man. About him is neither the glow of heaven nor the sheen of Eden. He was neither priest, prophet, nor prince. He was a wealthy man, and his wealth came to him presumably by application of native intelligence and ingenuity. He was a husband, father, and friend. In short, he was (as MacLeish presented him in modern dress two millennia later) a self-made man, pure in heart, not particularly introspective or speculative, until his trouble began. This was the man whom God chose for a divine demonstration—a bourgeois *tyrannos*.

Magnitude is the problem. But, declares Arthur Miller, "In this stretching and tearing apart of the cosmos, in the very action of so doing, the character gains 'size,' the tragic stature which is spuriously attached to the royal or high born in our minds. The commonest of men may take on that stature." [26] Thus Job suggests an American interpretation of the words of the anonymous Gentleman in *King Lear*, who, shocked by the spectacle of madness in a monarch, cries: "A sight most pitiful in the meanest wretch,/ Past speaking of in a king" (IV, vi, 208–209). In a democratic society, the meanest wretch may count for a king.

Job is arbitrarily thrust into an ironic *agon* of the Innocent Tyrannos versus the Omnipotent Force, an act understood by American tragedians, whose vision is still darkened by residual Calvinism. Countless words have been written throughout the centuries on this *agon*, even in America. Of all these essays, I have chosen Josiah Royce's attempt to resolve the irony, because Royce is in the American tradition

26. Arthur Miller, "Tragedy and the Common Man," in Richard Levin (ed.), *Tragedy: Plays, Theory, and Criticism* (New York: Harcourt, Brace, 1960), 172.

of practical idealism that includes both Emerson and William James. Royce perceives a covenant of suffering between God and man, in which man is fated to complete God: "Without suffering, without ill, without woe, evil, tragedy, God's life could not be perfected. . . . It is logically necessary that the Captain of your salvation should be perfect through [your] suffering." [27] To a philosopher, this necessity may be logical; to a tragedian, it is merely evident.

For a hero simply to endure suffering would result in melodrama. The Book of Job exemplifies the search for a teleology of suffering. Job suffers because he rejects the alternatives offered by wife and friends. His wife's suggestion is desperate and conclusive: "Curse God, and die!" (2:9). Simple and easy, but to Job completely unacceptable. He is too strong for that. Once, long before, the biblical Adam yielded to his wife's invitation to sin. But that was in another age and in another country, and under a different set of circumstances. Adam's strength lay in rejecting the peace of Eden and choosing the suffering of sin and death; Job's strength lay in rejecting the peace of sin and death and choosing the suffering of remaining under God's eye.

When his friends heard about Job's plight, "they came every one from his place," anxious to help. They offered a new alternative: Admit iniquity and thus reason out the suffering, for therein lies the peace of the soul. Limited in their vision, wrote A. B. Davidson, the friends expound upon "the theory that sin and suffering are in all cases connected." Only Job insists that this notion is naïve, that this is a "theory of providence which cannot be harmonized with the facts observed in the world." [28] Not only does Job

27. Josiah Royce, "The Problem of Evil," in Richard Hone (ed.), *Voice Out of the Whirlwind: The Book of Job* (San Francisco: Chandler, 1960), 243.
28. A. B. Davidson, "Introduction to the Book of Job," *ibid.*, 71–72.

commend himself to the American mind as a self-made man, but his test of a new idea is his experience, a criterion dear to our native way of thinking. As a true tyrannos, therefore, Job exercises his freedom of the will to stand and declare his righteousness. Indeed, the whole point of the enactment is that he was chosen as its protagonist because God knew in His predictive vision that this is what Job would choose. Of all in the dramatis personae, only Job displayed the personality to make the choice that Gad had fated him to make.

It was not his proverbial patience, but his unique steadfastness, his unshakable belief in his own integrity, that compelled him to both believe and question God Himself. "Though he slay me," he cries out, "yet will I trust in Him; but I will maintain mine own ways before Him" (13:15). True worship, to the author of the Book of Job, is not man groveling before God, admitting to uncommitted sin. True worship is man, in Arthur Miller's words, "demanding his right."

All along Job wanted one thing: "Oh that one would hear me! behold my desire is, that the Almighty would answer me" (31:35). And he succeeds. As Laurence Michel says, "Job is God's champion. . . . His purpose is to cry out loud and long, and not be silenced; his passion is to argue down his comforters, at the imminent danger of sinning by mere vehemence with his mouth; and he actually succeeds in talking God down out of his heaven." [29] That God pays attention to a common-born, persistent tyrannos is a point not lost on American tragedians.

Job's cry, George Steiner argues, is into the question of divine justice: "This demand for justice is the pride and burden of the Judaic tradition" which is satisfied by the

29. Laurence Michel, "The Possibility of a Christian Tragedy," in Laurence Michel and Richard Sewall (eds.), *Tragedy: Modern Essays in Criticism* (Englewood Cliffs, N.J.: Prentice-Hall, 1963), 222.

reward Job receives in the epilogue.[30] Yet, for Steiner, the reward destroys the tragic essence of the book. I think, however, that Steiner is wrong on two counts. First, the Judaic tradition insists upon justice only in the human sphere; when God is involved, Judaism insists upon faith in divine purpose—that is, in an ultimate justice that we cannot perceive. Secondly, largess in the epilogue is no surety against a rehearsal of tragedy for a Job in the next generation; after all, Job himself had been rich before and what did it get him? Justice and manifest reward are not the questions at all; they are external to tragedy. Tragedians do not concern themselves with justice on a cosmic plane, but only with the way life is down here.

Down here, the tyrannos does not question either the justice or the power of God. "I own thy speechless, placeless power," cries Ahab to the corposants, the fiery representations of omnipotence (*Moby-Dick*, Chapter 119), and Ahab's cry carries through all American tragedies of the tyrannos. This covenant of tragedy demands that the hero go on a voyage of discovery of the consequences of his heroic nature. The undertaking is as fated as the Omnipotent's response. In the Book of Job, the hero, as he must, asks not for justice but for knowledge. God, as He must, answers a righteous demand for knowledge not with reason but with power. God's voice out of the whirlwind is a thunderous review of His omniscience and omnipotence and eternality. The Lord correctly taunts Job with his limitations. Job's tragedy leads to a catharsis wherein we pity him for his suffering and frustration, and we are terror-stricken because God's answer is no answer at all, and we are left with the vast void of wonder.

In the final tableau, the virtuous, steadfast tyrannos

30. George Steiner, *The Death of Tragedy* (1961; reprint, New York: Hill and Wang, 1963), 4.

stands in the posture of "triumphant ignominy" (Hawthorne's description in *The Scarlet Letter* of the end of
Arthur Dimmesdale). He says to the Lord, "Behold I am
vile; what shall I answer thee? I will lay my hand upon my
mouth" (40:4). Thus, Job became "father to all tragedy,"
wrote Richard Sewall, "where the stress is on the inner
dynamics of man's response to destiny."

The Book of Job is significant to American tragedy not
only because of the hero and the theme, but also because of
the pattern of the drama. First of all, it modifies the Aristotelian plot. The principle of peripety is conspicuous here
by its being violated. The descent into catastrophe is visited
upon the hero early in the drama and comes not from inner
frailty or error of judgment. The Book of Job shifts attention from the spectacle of catastrophe based on plot to one
based on emotional Sturm und Drang and spiritual climax.
This sort of plot is characteristic of American tragedy. Secondly, the shift of emphasis in the plot refocuses our conventional view of protagonist and antagonist in tragedy.
Usually, the protagonist is clearly a hero, and the antagonist
strives villainously against him. But who is the antagonist of
Job? In the Book of Job the conflict is actually between Job
on one side and his beloved wife and friends on the other.
They are the tempters who work to dissuade Job from his
fated role in the tragedy as the special champion of God's
will. How painful it is to witness the mistaken love of Job's
antagonists and his ineluctable refusal of their help. More
and more, episode by episode, he recedes into isolation.

"God delights to isolate us every day," wrote Emerson in
1844, when he was just beginning his philosophical change
from unadulterated optimism to forced recognition of the
presence of tragedy in the world. "[He] hides from us past
and future. We would look about us, but with grand polite-
ness he draws down before us an impenetrable screen of

purest sky, and another behind us of purest sky." [31] This may serve as a summation of the theme of the Book of Job.

Thus, in theme, form, and concept of tragic heroism, the Book of Job anticipates and codifies American tragedy. For one eminent American tragedian, Arthur Miller, the story of Job is the authoritative example of realistic tragedy that balances the authority of classical tragedy: "The Greeks could probe the heavenly origin of their ways and confirm the rightness of laws. And Job could face God in anger, demanding his right, and end in submission." Miller affirmed the life of both tragic traditions in an essay he entitled "Tragedy and the Common Man," [32] the publication of which, significantly, preceded the production of his drama about a modern tyrannos, Willy Loman. Thus the modern tyrannos is sanctified by the biblical tradition as he receives his literary authority from the Greek, a legacy to which I now turn.

THE PARADIGM OF OEDIPUS

Oedipus. Having uttered the name of that classic tragic hero, we have in the main (though not entirely, of course) summed up the heritage of classical tragedy in America. It is Oedipus against whom critics measure candidates for modern tragic heroism like Faulkner's Joe Christmas and Miller's Willy Loman.[33] And when Krutch in "The Tragic Fallacy" is not invoking Shakespeare to contrast with mod-

31. Whicher (ed.), *Selections from Emerson*, 265.
32. Miller, "Tragedy and the Common Man," 172.
33. John L. Longley, Jr., *Tragic Mask: A Study of Faulkner's Heroes* (Chapel Hill: University of North Carolina Press, 1963); John Gassner, "Tragic Perspectives: A Series of Queries," in John D. Hurrell (ed.), *Two Modern American Tragedies* (New York: Scribner's, 1961); Thomas Lask, "How Do You Like Willy Loman?" New York *Times*, January 30, 1966, Sec. 2, p. 23; Richard J. Foster, "Confusion and Tragedy: The Failure of Miller's Salesman," in Hurrell (ed.), *Two Modern American Tragedies*, 82–88.

ern tragedians, he is conjuring up Sophocles, which means *Oedipus.*

He also figures prominently in essays by two modern American tragedians: Maxwell Anderson in *The Essence of Tragedy* (1939) and Arthur Miller in his introduction to his *Collected Plays* (1957). Invoking Sophocles as first in tragedy, Maxwell Anderson extrapolates from him an overview of Greek influence on modern theater:

> Our theatre has followed the Greek pattern with no change in essence. . . . We sometimes follow Sophocles, whose tragedy is always an exaltation of the human spirit, sometimes Euripides whose tragi-comedy follows the same pattern of an excellence achieved through suffering. The forms of both tragedy and comedy have changed a good deal in non-essentials, but in essentials—and especially in the core of meaning which they have for audiences—they are in the main the same religious rites which grew up around the altars of Attica long ago.[34]

What Anderson means to tell us, I think, is that modern theater still is religious in the sense that it is concerned with man's relationship to an external power. This "religious affirmation," Anderson finds, is woven into all works that are "dedicated to man's aspiration, to his kinship with the gods, to his unending, blind attempt to lift himself above his lusts and pure animalism." [35] And Oedipus looms as the hero who has made familiar the characteristics of the tyrannos— *arete*, the heroic impulse that must be fed; *hubris*, the pride that goeth before his fall; *hamartia*, the hero's flaw; finally, *dike*, the law of submission to the omnipotent. In these traits, the concept of Greek fate is betokened.

One caveat is vital here: we must realize that Greek tragedy was read in America with Christian-conditioned eyes.

34. Maxwell Anderson, *The Essence of Tragedy and Other Footnotes and Papers* (1939; reprint, New York: Russell and Russell, 1970), 12.
35. *Ibid.,* 14.

All aspects of the influence of these plays on American literature—the idea of fate, the nature of the hero, the design of the plot—must be seen in the light of the circumstance that first came the Bible, then came Greek drama. Even one of today's most influential classical scholars, H. D. F. Kitto, speaking of "the great god Apollo" in a discussion of one of the plays in which this character appears, writes, "We may unconsciously assume a degree of 'godliness' which is not there, so ingrained in us is the idea of a personal, beneficent god." He calls the end of *Prometheus Bound* a "crucifixion scene," [36] conjuring up all the moral paradoxes and implications that surround the primal Christian tragedy. Certainly this attitude is not foreign to less scholarly, but perhaps more sensitive, readers of classical tragedy, the modern tragic writers themselves. That is why Anderson speaks of religious affirmation in theater today. It is what accounts for the automatic commingling of Christian and Greek symbolic meanings in the heroism of Ahab, Mio Romagna, Clyde Griffiths, Lavinia and Orin Mannon, and Joe Christmas. It is an American interpretation of fate.

Fate in Greek tragedy is given to us as the manifestation of a supernal power without apparent room for human glorification. This is what underlies the definition of tragedy in the 1934 second edition of *Webster's New International Dictionary*: "The action as a whole is conceived as a manifestation of fate, in which the characters are somewhat passively involved." Nietzsche's definition of Greek tragic vision had gone one step further. He describes Greek tragedy as "a will to tragedy, profound pessimism." [37] This pessimism, say Cleanth Brooks and Robert Heilman in a famed textbook on the drama, might easily be shared by the read-

36. H. D. F. Kitto, *Greek Tragedy* (1950; reprint, London: Methuen, 1966), 135.
37. Friedrich Nietzsche, *The Birth of Tragedy*, trans. Francis Golffing (1872; reprint, Garden City, N.Y.: Doubleday, 1956), 8.

er who "tends to ask what Oedipus [the perennial example] could have done to avoid the fate which overtakes him and, if he can find no such preventive step indicated, he feels that Oedipus is simply a passive, helpless victim of fate." [38] In American terms, Greek tragedy sounds like a harbinger of seventeenth-century Calvinism and twentieth-century naturalism.

The earliest American approach to the concept of fate, under the guise of Calvinistic predeterminism, was to equate fate with evil. As a counterclaim in the early part of the nineteenth century, the idea of fate was temporarily suspended. In William Ellery Channing's first trumpeting of transcendentalism and in Emerson's essays in the 1830s and early 1840s, a notion of fate was largely absent—quite in keeping with their insistence that evil was literally nothing to talk about; it was merely the absence of good.

But the corrective was not long in coming. In 1851–52 in his essay on "Fate," Emerson set the policy on this matter for American tragedy. He admits that since the era of the Puritans, America had dealt with "superficialness" because her philosophers failed to face up to evil. "Great men, great nations have not been boasters and buffoons, but perceivers of the tenor of life, and have manned themselves to face it." Over the centuries, he says, man has recognized the belt of fate around him, and "the Greek tragedy" expressed the idea. " 'Whatever is fated, that will take place. The great immense mind of Jove is not to be transgressed.' " Against this supernal power, man's resistance "looks so ridiculously inadequate." [39]

Yet, "if you believe in Fate to your harm," Emerson im-

38. Cleanth Brooks and Robert B. Heilman, *Understanding Drama: Twelve Plays* (New York: Holt, 1948), 580.
39. Whicher (ed.), *Selections from Emerson*, 331, 332, 338.

plores as the transition to the second half of his essay, "believe it at least for your good." [40] And we are off once more on an Emersonian flight of practical idealism that is propelled from his Christian belief in the morality of cosmic governance. There is a constant *agon* between fate and what Emerson calls power. Fate is supernal, deterministic, objective, evil, and painful; power is human, individualistic, active, free, and optimistic. Emerson recognizes the reasons for fatalistic resignation, but he is severely impatient with it. He calls for a counteraction by humanity. Fate, like pain, is but a moral test. Great nations, Emerson has told us, "have *manned* themselves" to face fate (italics mine). The definition of man, then, seems to call for a heroic resistance to the inroads of fate. In our terms, what Emerson calls for is an American tyrannos.

How vital Emerson's concept of fate is in American tragedy can already be anticipated. During his lifetime, a new "naturalism," a modern surrogate term for fate, began to be reflected in literature. In the later onslaught of Darwin, Marx, and Freud, American literature—and its tragedies as well—stood on the terrible brink of enervating its heroes into a nonheroic condition even beyond antiheroism. That American literature did not become a demonstration of human passivity is due to Emerson's philosophical and religious brush-clearing.

It will not do to try to avoid the modern reader's moral predicament, as Rosalind Barstow suggests: "[The modern reader] is apt to worry about Greek 'fatalism' and the justice of the downfall of Oedipus, and finding no satisfactory solution for these intellectual difficulties, loses half the pleasure the drama was intended to produce. Perhaps we trouble ourselves too much concerning the Greek notions of fate

40. *Ibid.*, 340.

in human life." [41] Her statement is, I submit, quite incomprehensible. First of all, it is asking too much to suggest not only a suspension of disbelief when we read plays about anthropomorphic gods and creaky cosmic machinery, but also a suspension of belief in some kind of equilibrium of goodness and reward, evil and justice, that we have been nurtured on. Secondly, Greek plays commend themselves to us today simply because they *do* ask questions about fate and relationship to deity, questions that we ourselves ask, knowing no one can answer them. How else can a modern audience relate to a play that seemingly, in C. M. Bowra's summation, "shows the humbling is not deserved; it is not a punishment for insolence, nor in the last resort is it due to any fault of judgment or character in the man. The gods display their power because they will." [42] Miss Barstow would do as well to suggest that we do not worry too much about Calvinism in *The Scarlet Letter* or naturalism in *An American Tragedy*.

Like the biblical Job, Oedipus is god-beset and god-provoking. Bernard Knox observes that "Oedipus, the independent being, was a perfectly appropriate subject for the demonstration" of the power of the gods, and he equates him with Job, "another great figure who served as the subject of a divine demonstration." [43] Oedipus was an appropriate subject for tragedy precisely for the same reason that Job was. He had the endowed qualities that the supernal deity needed at that particular moment. We see here again the Jobite covenant of tragedy. "The gods are not directing events as if from the outside," Kitto avers. "They work *in* the events." There is a precarious balance between external control and inner causality that precludes the conclu-

41. Marjorie Barstow, "Oedipus Rex as the Ideal Hero of Aristotle," in Levin (ed.), *Tragedy*, 181.
42. C. M. Bowra, "From *Sophoclean Tragedy*," *ibid.*, 185.
43. Knox, "Sophocles' Oedipus," 22.

sion that "an inexorable destiny or a malignant god is guiding the events." [44] Oedipus' nature is precisely such that his line of action fulfills the prediction of the oracle, as Job fulfills the Lord's expectations. There is really no point in asking if there were another choice such a hero could have made. Arthur Miller makes a facetious, but incisive *reductio ad absurdum* regarding *Oedipus Tyrannos*: "[Oedipus] must surely decide to divorce [Jocasta], provide for their children, firmly resolve to investigate the family background of his next wife, and thus deprive us of a very fine play and the name for a famous neurosis." [45] The point is that the Christian ingredient in the reading of *Oedipus* makes the seed of tragedy grow in what is for us its proper soil: not in the action, but in the nature of the hero who is typically a fated independent tyrannos, as Oedipus was.

In dramaturgy as well, we hear echoes of the Book of Job in *Oedipus*. Again the theme of confrontation of man's search for knowledge, especially knowledge about one's self, is a form of action, tragic action. As in the Book of Job, the conflict is entirely between the hero who is the protagonist and the character who is his antagonist, not between the protagonist and superior force that originated the tragic action. The fated protagonist must reach his final catastrophic destination as the gods desire. He who stands in his way to that destination, he who in the guise of friendship or of enmity would alter the destiny decreed and predicted by the gods, is the true antagonist. In *Oedipus*, Tiresias is that antagonist, for he is the one who advises the hero to cease his lurching to the destiny the gods had planned. To place as antagonist the character who would keep the protagonist from pain is consummate irony.

44. Kitto, *Greek Tragedy*, 128, 139.
45. Arthur Miller, introduction to his *Collected Plays* (New York: Viking, 1957), 35.

As a man, Oedipus displays modern traits, and to American writers, is a tyrannos after our own dreaming. He climbed from a log cabin in Corinth to a palace in Thebes by his own wits in the way that will one day be classified as typically American. Oedipus in the play is not presumed by the Thebans to be of a blooded line. As far as they are concerned, he has come out of the wilderness, unknown but precocious, highly intelligent, and admirably opportunistic. No doubt he can be called an inspired pragmatist. Judging from Creon's attitude, he is not loved, but he is respected. He is the virtuous tyrannos par excellence, as Knox has asserted. Moreover, Cedric Whitman says that our popular interpretation of the play has been to suppose that the gods hated Oedipus and devised a horrible plot to punish him. But, Whitman goes on, "Sophocles, on the contrary, has painted him as a man willfully innocent, passionately honest in motive, and full of heroic *arete*," a term which is defined as "an inner impulse toward greatness, which makes a man a hero and drives him to expend himself in order to realize his internal 'law'." [46]

But *arete* carries within itself the cancer of its own destruction, for it leads to the classic sin of hubris. In the case of the archetype Oedipus, however, hubris can be defined as self-respect, self-fulfillment, and all the other virtues that are part of an individual's praiseworthy character. Where does *arete* end and hubris begin? It is a nice distinction. That distinction, however, must be made, and made in terms of a violation of a recognizable law of civilization or of society by a fated individual, who is then driven to catastrophe. This is the concept of *dike*, the cosmic law that is a "balance of forces of Nature," that operates like a "law of

---

46. Cedric H. Whitman, "From *Sophocles: A Study of Heroic Humanism*," in Levin (ed.), *Tragedy*, 191; see also Levin's note 4, p. 192.

averages," and that is "not necessarily Justice." [47] As the Book of Job and Emerson taught, morality in tragedy does not lie in the justice of the protagonist's destiny, but in the balance of law that is achieved. Arthur Miller signifies that the law of *dike* still lives by comparing the violation through ignorance of cosmic law by Oedipus and the violation through ignorance of social and personal law by his Willy Loman.[48] Catastrophe ensues. Equilibrium is all. Oedipus transcends the singular problems of Thebes, the horrible facts of his own life, the delimitations of Greek fate. He reaches that archetypal importance where one critic can state, "Oedipus is Everyman." [49]

EPHRAIM REX

"I'm always acutely conscious," said Eugene O'Neill, "of the Force behind—(Fate, God, our biological past creating our present, whatever one calls it—Mystery certainly)—and of the eternal tragedy of Man in his glorious, self-destructive struggle to make the Force express him instead of being, as an animal is, an infinitesimal incident in its happiness." [50] In this statement, O'Neill reveals the components of his tragic vision: Greeklike fate, a Calvinistic God, and popular Freudianism. The *agon* pits a tyrannos who tries to fulfill his nature against an omnipotent Other. The vehicle in which O'Neill first essayed a tragic plot was *Desire Under the Elms*, a truly American tragedy that translates—it does not transplant, as does *Mourning Becomes Electra*—past legacies of tragedy into modern expression.

The story of *Desire Under the Elms* (1924) involves an aged farmer, a wenchy stepmother (his third wife), and a

---

47. Kitto, *Greek Tragedy*, 135.   48. Miller, *Collected Plays*, 35.
49. Whitman, "From *Sophocles*," 194.
50. Quoted by Sophus K. Winther, *Eugene O'Neill: A Critical Study* (2nd ed.; New York: Russell and Russell, 1961), 220.

virile son by his dead second wife. The play takes place in New England, a region intoxicated with the will of God ever since Cotton Mather's time. Indeed, in the hands of O'Neill the cloud of this New England past hangs heavy over the action and serves as a tool by which he will attempt to aggrandize the stature of his tragic hero. Once again a common man labors under fate and God.

New England also means nature, the old Emersonian arena for man's education—tragic and otherwise—in spirit and self-reliance. Nature is represented in this play by two symbols. The first is described in the opening stage setting: "Two enormous elms are on each side of the house. They bend their trailing branches down over the roof. They appear to protect and at the same time subdue. There is a sinister maternity in their aspect, a crushing, jealous absorption. They have developed from their intimate contact with the life of man in the house an appalling humanness. They brood oppressively over the house." [51] The stage direction, though expressed with dollar-book Freudian implication, recalls precisely what nature came to mean in America's intellectual history: the promise and the tragedy.

The other symbol of nature in this play is the land. Land is permanent, the one thing to be depended upon in a life of flux and temporality; it transcends the tricks of time and history. One of the major motifs of the play is the ownership of the land, for ownership means passing the land on to progeny, outwitting death and weakness. Transcending the narrowness of mortality, the self can be fulfilled. So here stand the elms, the witches of time, drawing sustenance from the land, and the land itself, a perpetual challenge to the man who has the personality of a hero. Thus O'Neill tries

51. Eugene O'Neill, *Three Plays: Desire Under the Elms, Strange Interlude, Mourning Becomes Electra* (New York: Random House, n.d.), 2. References will hereafter be made in the text to this edition by act, scene, and page.

to veneer his plot with the setting and the context of magnitude.

Now O'Neill must fashion a character to befit the call and the challenge. We need a tyrannos, a figure who achieves nobility by the recognition of being chosen by fate and by his aspiration, ruthlessness, and steadfastness. What does the land mean to each of the dramatis personae in *Desire Under the Elms*? To Eben Cabot, the son, ownership means vindication of his mother and vengeance for her death; to Abbie, the young stepmother, the land means merely what every woman craves, security. Only Ephraim Cabot, the father, sees the land as more than merely a tool or a "purty" farm; only he perceives it as the visible sign of an inexorable power. Instinctively, Ephraim understands the demands made upon man by time and place.

Hard, unforgiving, and unrelenting, he is a kingly man to assume the human role in the encounter with fate. He is "tall and gaunt, with great, wiry, concentrated power"; but he carries the antithesis, the frailty of character necessary for the universality of the tragic protagonist: there is "a petty pride in [his] own narrow strength" (I, iv, 18). He—and only he—has both the hubris to respond when the call of God goes through the land and the *hamartia* to engender his own tragedy. It is upon his steadfast nature that God rests His heavy hand. The marks of Job and of Oedipus are upon Ephraim.

Because O'Neill is considered by some a Freudian naturalist, I suppose we ought to remark that Ephraim's inner drive for the land sublimates some unconscious compensatory drive. "The struggle used to be with the gods," O'Neill remarked, "but is now with himself, his own past, his attempt 'to belong'." [52] The Other in modern times is inter-

52. W. R. Thurman, "Journey Into Night: Elements of Tragedy in Eugene O'Neill," *Quarterly Journal of Speech*, LII (1966), 142.

nalized. But O'Neill's concept of the hero with a subconscious ought not to be seen as a particularized case history. His intention is to push his plots beyond the Freudian void. These complexes he equates with destiny,[53] not merely with individual destiny. Emotions to O'Neill are "not only of our individual experiences but of the experiences of the whole human race, back through the ages." [54] Quite clearly, then, O'Neill's intentions transcend the self, transcend the society and century of which his play is ostensibly an expression, and take on the veneer of an enactment of magnitude. As Krutch remarked, "The events [of this play] really occur out of place and out of time." [55]

Ephraim is transformed into the man who sees himself divinely chosen as the monarch of the land, on which, as far as he is concerned, his Puritan God still walks. And in the stones on the land, he encounters Him: "Waal—this place was nothin' but fields of stones. Folks laughed when I tuk it. They couldn't know what I knowed. When ye kin make corn sprout out o' stones, God's livin' in yew! They wa'n't strong enuf fur that! They don't laugh no more. Some died hereabouts. Some went West an' died. They're all under ground—fur follerin' arter an easy God. God hain't easy" (II, ii, 31). It does not matter that God was a quaint notion to O'Neill's sophisticated 1920s audience. What does matter is that Ephraim's psyche is so fashioned and fated that he accepts Him as alive, active, and paying attention. God may be "only an image of [Ephraim's] own ego," [56] and no long-

53. Doris Falk, *Eugene O'Neill and the Tragic Tension* (New Brunswick, N.J.: Rutgers University Press, 1958), 129.

54. Quoted by Mary B. Mullett, "Extraordinary Story of Eugene O'Neill," *American Magazine* (November, 1922), 34. See also Falk, *Eugene O'Neill and the Tragic Tension*, 16.

55. Joseph Wood Krutch, introduction to *Nine Plays by Eugene O'Neill* (New York: Modern Library, 1941), xvi.

56. Falk, *Eugene O'Neill and the Tragic Tension*, 95.

er a theological fact, but He is a psychological fact. That is truth enough for a modern tragedy.

Out of these concepts of regional and racial history O'Neill fashioned his tyrannos. Like Oedipus, Ephraim Cabot attempts mastery over his life and destiny and over the lives and destiny of those around him. And with rectitude! In him roils the nature that responded to the ineluctable election by God. After all, at the behest of this Voice, he did raise crops out of flinty soil, and like any king he did have sons to pass on the Lord's work. The covenant between God and Ephraim is clear.

This covenant O'Neill concretizes in a play that lurches toward peripety, anagnorisis, and catharsis, the eternal verities of tragedy left from Aristotle's *Poetics*. As far as peripety is concerned, *Desire Under the Elms* is a fine example of how this device *cannot* work in modern times as it classically did. Ephraim Cabot does not lose station, title, possessions, and power as Oedipus did. Wherein, then, is his peripety? O'Neill locates it where modern realism demands it to be: in the character of his hero. It is not the action depicting a reversal of fortune that interests O'Neill, but a peripety of mind and emotion. Ephraim learns that the child he thought was his has been murdered, that he has been cuckolded and shamed, that his wife and son are about to be incarcerated for murder:

> CABOT (*stares at them, his face hard. A long pause—vindictively*): Ye make a slick pair of murdering turtle doves! Ye'd ought t' be both hung on the same limb an' left thar t' swing in the breeze an' rot—a warning t' old fools like me t' b'ar their lonesomeness alone—an' fur young fools like ye t' hobble their lust (II, iv, 57).

Then O'Neill has Ephraim descend for a moment into an obscene weakness, toying with the idea of going west for easy gold and actually dancing a jig with the idea of it. The very contrast of this moment with the ruthless, relentless natural demeanor of Cabot emphasizes the great void of confusion and desperation in him. All seems lost—the planning, the years of lonesomeness and deprivation and disappointment. This is the peripety of this tyrannos. He is a man alone, beset by the anagnorisis of his own limitations and of the paradox that the power that set the enactment and placed him in the center of it is the same force that ironically snatches fulfillment from him. Ephraim Cabot learns that "life itself is nothing. It is the dream that keeps us fighting, willing—living." [57] Immediately, however, Ephraim recovers:

> Mebbe they's easy gold in the West but it hain't God's gold. It hain't fur me. I kin hear His voice warnin' me agen t' be hard an' stay on my farm. I kin see his hand usin' Eben t' steal [my hidden money] t' keep me from weakness. I kin feel I be in the palm of His hand. His fingers guidin' me. (*A pause —then he mutters sadly*) It's a-goin' t' be lonesomer now than ever it war afore—an' I'm gittin' old, Lord—ripe on the bough . . . [ellipsis O'Neill's] (*Then stiffening*) Waal—what d'ye want? God's lonesome, hain't He? God's hard and lonesome!
> (II, iv, 57–58)

John Mason Brown once said, "Though [O'Neill] possesses the tragic vision, he cannot claim the tragic tongue." [58] Perhaps. But the very inarticulation, the strangled accents, do express the same perception of God's determinism and purpose as the dying speeches of older tyrannoi. The lack of Ephraim Cabot's grandiloquence may very well increase the pathos and the stark dignity of a man denuded of his hopes.

The dramaturgical challenge that O'Neill faced is the same one that faced all tragedians whose heroes are tyrannoi. How can one engender the necessary sympathy so that peripety will be accepted, not as the justified end of a hate-

57. Quoted by Mullett, "Extraordinary Story," 119.
58. Quoted by F. I. Carpenter, *Eugene O'Neill* (New York: Twayne, 1964), 169.

fully prideful, cruel, and maniacal character, but as the inevitable end of a character of nobility? To fail to do so is to destroy the catharsis, as Aristotle posited when he precluded villains from the possibility of tragic heroism. And Ephraim Cabot's character is no help: he is cruel, overbearing, lustful, hypocritical, prideful, and egocentric. Yet we are meant to feel that all of these characteristics are necessary for the historical design into which he has been preordained. We see that his hubris is the quality that will at once fulfill his destiny and destroy his design. His relentless steadfastness to his vision is what embitters his character for us and yet conceives our admiration for him. We recognize in Ephraim Cabot what we learned from Job: steadfastness is the quality by which an ungodly godlike man attracted the attention of the "Force behind."

Pity and terror are aroused when we see this man's world crash in shards about him; and to hear him admit his age and condition, we join the human sufferer as Stephen Dedalus said, in pity for his human sufferings. It is also a moment of terror to envision, together with the tyrannos, the ironic machinations of—as Stephen called it—the secret cause. Finally, we thrill to his refusal to bow. "A man wills his own defeat when he pursues the unattainable," said O'Neill. "But the struggle is his success. . . . Such a figure is necessarily tragic, but to me he is exhilarating." [59] It is the characteristic end of a tragedy of a tyrannos. Thus O'Neill infuses nobility into a most common and dislikable character, fulfilling the not-so-incompatible demands of tragic and realistic theater.

THREE GREEK EPISODES

Speaking of O'Neill's *Mourning Becomes Electra*, Louis Martz remarked, "This family curse [of the Mannons] has been shipped in from Greece and has never quite settled

59. *Ibid.*, 176.

down in New England." [60] Something like that can be said
as well of the transplantation of Greek fate in the form of
naturalism in Theodore Dreiser's *An American Tragedy*
and of Greeklike godly caprice in Maxwell Anderson's
Winterset. These three Greek imports violate the insistence
in American tragedy that the hero and the gods must reach
an equilibrium. These authors try to create tyrannoi, but
leave us only melodramatic heroes to weep over. Because
so much power is bestowed upon the external force and so
little left for the hero, and because Greek tragedy has en-
snared these authors into being so obviously derivative, one
wonders if these tragedies are American at all, regardless of
setting.

   Mourning Becomes Electra (1931) is at once a grander
tragedy and yet a narrower one than *Desire Under the Elms*.
The transcendence into universality in *Desire Under the
Elms* arose naturally out of time and place; in *Mourning* it
must arise initially from a prior knowledge of classical myth
and tragedy, specifically the curse upon the house of Atreus
as interpreted by Euripides, a more psychologically oriented
playwright than Aeschylus.[61] The setting clearly suggests
the Greek scene and visually thrusts out the first impression
of magnitude: "The house is placed back on a slight rise of
ground about three hundred feet from the street. It is a
large building of the Greek temple type that was the vogue

   60. Louis Martz, "The Saint as Tragic Hero," in Brooks (ed.), *Tragic
Themes in Western Literature*, 155.
   61. For the influence of Aeschylus, see, among many, Lionel Trilling,
"Eugene O'Neill," in Walter Meserve (ed.), *Discussions of American Drama*
(Boston: Heath, 1965), 23, and W. A. Geier, "Images of Man in Five American Dramatists" (Ph.D. dissertation, Vanderbilt University, 1959), Chap. 1.
I opt for a stronger influence from Euripides, because O'Neill's structure
and theme seem closer. Electra is truly a protagonist, with a longer part and
more influential action by far than the Electras of either Aeschylus or Sophocles; the underlying theme of incest is more manifest in Euripides' version,
intermixed with the theme of revenge; and the question of justice within
fate is more broadly handled by Euripides than by the others.

in the first half of the nineteenth century" ("General Scene of the Trilogy," 224).

There is more to the leap of time than suggesting the ancient Greek theme and the immediate time of the play as the last century. O'Neill wants the setting to intimidate the present occupants of the mansion as it did previous generations: *"Behind the driveway the white Grecian temple portico with its six tall columns extends across the stage"* (Stage setting, "Homecoming," 227).

The atmosphere of the portentous past exudes from these pillars as it did from the elms that framed the setting of O'Neill's other tragedy. Thus the pillars underline the story and theme of the trilogy. In the transplantation of the house of Atreus, O'Neill intimates that the tragedies of old are part of our racial and individual experience; that they transcend time and distance; that they are part of our cyclical history, because, after all, human nature has not changed very much. Especially in New England, man is a fated and determined breed. For O'Neill, the curse of the house of Atreus becomes the curse of besmirched ancestry, an inescapable history, and a runaway subconscious, all descriptions of antiquity's concept of fate.

Especially concerned with the subconscious, O'Neill used popularized Freudianism in *Mourning Becomes Electra* as a new "secret cause." His story of Lavinia Mannon is an obvious syndrome of the ego caught between pleasure desired and reality denied, between the fulfillment of a socially obnoxious wish and the placation of the unsatisfied id by formulating a compromise based on a facade called "justice." [62]

Moreover, O'Neill compresses the audience into the dilemma of ego and id. Our instincts want freedom for the

---

62. See Frederick J. Hoffman, *Freudianism and the Literary Mind* (1945; reprint, Baton Rouge: Louisiana State University Press, 1957), Chap. 1.

adulterous lovers, yet social reality cannot have it so, and we know it. We dislike Lavinia in her role as an avenging agent because she is demonic and because her justice is compensation for unsatisfied lust, but we also agree that the guilty must be punished. The superego works on us as it did upon Lavinia and her brother Orin. We learn with them that there is no escape. When O'Neill symbolizes the last abortive fling at escape in the romantic dreamworld of the Blessed Isles with dark, dusky maidens and demigods cavorting in pagan license, he will have us realize that responsibility for guilt simply waited until Lavinia and Orin came back to the place of their encounter with the external power. In the manner of the ancient gods, Freud offered both the compulsions that initiated the tragedy and the Furies that executed it.

The superego is represented by another surrogate for the Olympian gods—the ancestral Puritan ghosts of the Mannon family. They represent the same oppressive power. But to Americans including O'Neill, Puritan ancestry connotes two further oppressions—religion and history. The coalescence of the Greek and the Christian is noted by Christine Mannon: "Each time I come back after being away it appears more like a sepulchre! The 'whited' one of the Bible—Pagan temple front stuck like a mask on Puritan gray ugliness! It was just like old Abe Mannon to build such a monstrosity—as a temple for his hatred" ("Homecoming," I, 237).

Through the scenic representation of Greek fate and Hebraic relentlessness, O'Neill begins to engender terror in his unfolding tragedy. Magnitude is assured. It is the special role of the family motif to emphasize the terror of history. Early in the play we learn that the Mannons of the past have committed the crimes of denial of love and of hypocrisy about their vaunted purity and status. Into this family

Lavinia is born, among their ghosts she was reared, and now she must take on the curse they left—a curse worked out in terms of denial of love and of hypocrisy. Even physically, the Mannons intrude upon the current cycle of time. Their brooding portraits hang in the sitting room, one a Mannon of "the witch-burning era," another of Revolutionary times, a third of the generation just prior to Ezra Mannon's. Moreover, these ghosts of the past intrude upon the present by replication in a living Mannon, again emphasizing the inescapability of history. Orin's face *"bears a striking resemblance to that of the portrait above him and [to his] dead [father's]"* ("The Hunted," III, stage setting, 303). When Orin murders his cousin Adam Brant, he stares into the face of the corpse and cries out, "By God, he does look like Father! . . . He looks like me, too! Maybe I've committed suicide!" ("The Hunted," IV, 332).

The ultimate irony of historical power—one can almost hear the dead Mannons laughing—comes in the final play of the trilogy. Driven by guilt-feelings that he had caused his beautiful mother to commit suicide, feelings that no amount of argument, escape, or rationalization by and with Lavinia can assuage, Orin has just proposed an incestuous union to his sister to preserve secrecy, compensate for the crime, and round off the curse of the Mannons: "Perhaps you're Marie Brantome, eh? And you say there are no ghosts in this house?" ("The Haunted," III, 365). Ironically, Lavinia for the moment takes on the guise of a hated memory, a girl who unwittingly caused a cycle of injustice and inhumanity now being repeated.

Now that the dimensions of the tragedy have been flung beyond the confines of locale, family, individual, and point of time, O'Neill creates a tyrannos to equal the demands of the action. For this, Sophocles, rather than Euripides, is the better teacher. Like Oedipus, who completely mistakes his role in the cause and cure of the plague, Lavinia uses her personality, ingenuity, and egoism to set herself up as justiciar of the Mannons, yet unwittingly the cause of her family's present plague. Before our eyes stalks the tyrannos, like Ephraim Cabot before her, dispensing hardness, maniacal justice, relentless wisdom. One by one she establishes mastery over all those around her—her mother through blackmail, Adam Brant through treachery, and Orin through cajolery. Lavinia becomes a lost psyche, a grotesque, denying her womanhood, seeing herself as a tyrannos destined to answer the call of her ancestors.

By portraying Lavinia's Freudian dilemma in terms of larger concepts of fate, O'Neill hoped to arouse the necessary sympathy for his tragic tyrannos. That Lavinia is a victim of self and time is evident throughout the trilogy, but never more so than when she appears in the last play like her mother reborn, beautiful, vibrant, and adventuresome. It is her last flicker of life. Pity is somewhat aroused here and perhaps deepened later when her friend Hazel Niles says to Lavinia:

> . . . I know you're suffering, Vinnie—and I know your conscience will make you do what's right—and God will forgive you. (*She goes quickly behind the lilacs and around the house to the rear.*)

But her reply to Hazel erodes what pity we might feel for Lavinia:

> (*looks after her and calls defiantly*) I'm not asking God or anybody for forgiveness. I forgive myself! (*She leans back and closes her eyes again—bitterly*) I hope there is a hell for the good somewhere! ("The Haunted," IV, 372)

This last is a bit of petulant defiance, far beneath the grandiosity O'Neill intended for his heroine and is indicative of his fuzzy thinking about how to conclude Lavinia's heroic career.

The possibilities of a strong catharsis are lessened because Lavinia's character diminishes rather than grows as the trilogy ends. She is defeated. As she says to Peter Niles, her erstwhile fiancé, "Always the dead between! It's no good trying any more!" ("The Haunted," IV, 374). No authentic American tragic hero speaks this way. Doris Falk asserts that Lavinia accepts the guilt and responsibility which lead her to realize that the punishment for self-hatred must be self-inflicted; and through this acknowledgment the "moral order" is manifested.[63] I cannot agree. In the final speech, in which Lavinia rejects suicide (the escape of her mother and brother) and cries, "I've got to punish myself," she concludes, "I know they [all the Mannons] will see to it I live for a long time! It takes the Mannons to punish themselves for being born" ("The Haunted," IV, 374). There is no anagnorisis here. The end is fatalistically Greek. Lavinia seems to have achieved no insight into her moral condition, no knowledge of what she contributed to the family's latest catastrophes. Unlike our feelings about other tragic catastrophes, we feel this one is deserved.

Compare our response to what happens to Orin, for whom a kind of pity and even terror are aroused. The death of Orin represents the most radical departure from his Greek source that O'Neill wrote into his trilogy. Orestes was acquitted of his matricide, because the gods slated him to bring vengeance upon the husband-killer and adulteress, Clytemnestra. Orin Mannon, however, dies for driving to her death his mother, an adulteress and husband-killer, but also a destined character in a fated drama. The acquittal of Orestes by the Areopagus reconciles ethics, religion, and government. In O'Neill's conception, reconciliation is ef-

63. Falk, *Eugene O'Neill and the Tragic Tension*, 141, 143.

fected only by the suicide of Orin. O'Neill gives Orin alternatives: he can be persuaded by Lavinia that Christine's
death is justified, he can continue to live as Lavinia's guilty
conscience, he can recognize his own contribution to his
family's demise. Ancient Furies being today's anxieties and
ancient certainties about justice being today's quandaries,
his choice is almost inevitable. Because he perceives the
irony of his guilt (which Lavinia cannot in her own case),
he goes the way his mother went. He suffers not only self-
punishment, but self-knowledge. The account is balanced.
Greek fate and Hebraic morality are now satisfied in a single
act. Here is the possibility of catharsis that makes Orin a
greater tragic hero than his sister, though he is too weakly
drawn to be a tyrannos. At least he dies as an American hero
modifying Greek fate with the fillip of morality.

The same, however, cannot be said of Theodore Dreiser's
victim of relentless fate, Clyde Griffiths, in *An American
Tragedy* (1925). Never does he grow in self-knowledge or
express an insight. The story of Clyde Griffiths is about
America and the catastrophic effect that its worship of the
bitch goddess success had upon its youth. The betrayal of
the ideals of the original American dream and of its youth-
ful dreamers is a chief theme of many writers of the 1920s,
but it is also the culmination of hints we have noticed in
Emerson's writings seventy-five years before. Dreiser is not
satisfied with the magnitude of a plot that portrays merely
American society. He wants nothing less than to capture in
modern settings a vision of the governance of men's lives by
unassailable external forces. For the Greek concept of fate,
he held the notion of chemisms; and for the Furies—heredity, environment, and chance. The Greek *deus ex machina*
became simply the machine, and Greek heroism against
destiny became the panting after success. For Greek gods
whose governance was the nature of nature, Dreiser gives

us Darwin, Freud, and Karl Marx. Instead of Sophocles or Euripides, he preferred Émile Zola. The contexts are different, but the same sense of uncontrollable, capricious power prevails. What the novel lacks is a tragic hero.

Prior to *An American Tragedy*, Dreiser had tried in dramatic form what he considered a tragedy, *The Hand of the Potter* (1918). From a letter to his friend H. L. Mencken, we glimpse the extent of his tragic vision: "If you would look at the title page you would see it [*Hand of the Potter*] is labeled *a tragedy*. What has tragedy ever illuminated unless it is the inscrutability of life and its forces and accidents?" [64] The vision is transcendent, far beyond the mere social forces that surround his characters, far beyond the naturalism that marks the hero. Dreiser evidently believes that the perfectability of society (even were it possible) would not bring individual freedom from fate. There is a power out there that will not be satiated, for it is inscrutable and operates through force and accident to wreak its will. Clearly, in *An American Tragedy* Dreiser is attempting a "naturalistic tragedy," depending upon the Darwinian and Freudian scientific rationale. [65] The story begins with dusk on a summer night, and the wide-angle lens of Dreiser's camera pans down into a city of 400,000. The city is significantly nameless in Chapter 1, for as far as the accident of Clyde's birth into it and into his family is concerned, it doesn't make any difference. At once we are made to feel that the sordid story about to ensue represents but the piece of an iceberg above the water. It is only the merest implication of the destructive power beneath.

That world, as has been said repeatedly, is to Dreiser a tinsel world, with reachable but ungraspable goals. And

64. Quoted in John J. Von Szeliski, "Dreiser's Experiment with Tragic Drama," *Twentieth Century Literature*, XII (1966), 32.
65. *Ibid.*, 31.

poor Clyde Griffiths is chosen for the enactment that will prove precisely that. At one point in the novel appears the following passage: "Of all the influences which might have come to Clyde at this time, either as an aid or an injury to his development, perhaps the most dangerous for him considering his temperament was this same Green-Davidson [Hotel]" in which he is surrounded by untouchable gaudiness and wealth (61).[66] In Dreiser's naturalistic view, great forces coagulate into petty actions. The die is cast, and once again the external power is conjoined with the temperament of the hero to form the covenant of a tragic enactment.

But it is the cosmic potential of the plot, not the heroism of the protagonist, that Dreiser emphasizes. Clyde is driven like the proverbial autumn leaf. The baleful influences of heredity and environment are now joined by chance, the third sibyl of fate. Clyde chances to become employed at the club where his uncle from Lycurgus, New York, is stopping, and he chances to meet that uncle. For a while, the logical consequences of heredity, environment, and chance take over the story. As Clyde moves from the Midwest to his uncle's factory in New York, a sense of inevitability as heavy as a Greek exercise in the depiction of fate hangs over the story, aided and abetted by the ponderous and stately style of Theodore Dreiser.

In his new locale Clyde meets Roberta, the representative of the have-nots, and Sonia, the delectable symbol of the haves. Never as sharply as now is the difference brought home to poor Clyde. Roberta becomes pregnant, and the dangerous influences of fate flow toward the climax. Seemingly, alternatives are offered to Clyde, or are they? Is it possible that he shall marry Roberta and settle down to a

66. Theodore Dreiser, *An American Tragedy*, intro. Alfred Kazin (1925; reprint, New York: Bantam, 1959). Page references in parentheses are to this edition.

life of underprivileged ignominy? Absurd—as absurd as the alternative Arthur Miller facetiously offered Oedipus. Is it possible that he shall, after all, effect an escape after the crime? Absurd—as absurd as expecting the Olympian gods to relent during one of their games of tragedy. The initiation of the climactic action and the consequences have long been planned. Emphasizing the irony, Philip Gerber said that Clyde is "driven to choose [murder] in order to open the road from Thorpe Street to Wykeagy Avenue." [67]

Dreiser's tragic vision cannot allow a human action to become truly self-operative, just as the gods carefully narrow any alternative left to Oedipus. Relating the climactic incident of Roberta and Clyde in the rowboat on Great Bittern Lake, Dreiser invokes a "genii at the *accidental* [my italics] rubbing of Aladdin's lamp . . . [which is] the very substance of some leering and diabolical wish or wisdom concealed in [Clyde's] own nature, and that now abhorrent and yet compelling, leering and yet intriguing, friendly and yet cruel, offered him a choice between an evil which threatened to destroy him, and a second evil which . . . still provided for freedom and success and love" (496). This sly serpentine inner voice is the voice of his natural inheritance: "some darker or primordial and unregenerate nature of his own." Passively, Clyde sits, enervated by the one glimpse into the black void of nature.

But immobility is no escape from the influences. Roberta rises in the boat to cross to him; she reaches for him; he tries to escape her touch, "but not even then with intention to do other than free himself of her." She is struck by the camera that he "still unconsciously held tight," and Clyde rises "half to assist or recapture her and half to apologize for the unintended blow." The boat capsizes and Roberta sinks. "And then the voice at his ear" convinces him that "this—

67. Philip Gerber, *Theodore Dreiser* (New York: Twayne, 1964), 138.

has been done for you. An accident—an accident—an unintentional blow on your part" has erased the blot on his future (526–27).

Heredity, environment, and chance—that is, the totality of fate—are not only interested and aware powers; they are mocking powers as well. Refusing to allow Clyde an escape through passivity from killing Roberta, they now refuse to allow an escape from the legal consequences of their machinations. He falls into the hands of prosecutors and defense attorneys who see him exactly as the gods had seen him—a nonentity, a toy, a tool. The capture, trial, Mrs. Griffiths' appeals, Clyde's death-house stay, and his execution take fully 250 pages to relate, to complete a total of more than 800 pages from first dusk to last. And all we have after so much excruciating detail about Clyde's life is a big zero. In circular fashion, the story ends where it began. Dusk, evening, a big city, a little boy with a glimmer of hope the faintest bit brighter than Clyde's.

Dreiser's dependence upon the cosmic scope of his plot is so evident in extent of vision and in depth of detail that Robert Penn Warren sees the accretion of fact in *An American Tragedy* as "the transliteration of logic into a poetry of destiny." We are drawn into the story, not through identification with a destined hero, but by witnessing the process of capricious and inscrutable fate. The reader of this novel, Warren says, "live[s] a destiny painfully waiting for a doom. We live into Clyde's doom, and in the process live our own secret sense of doom which is the backdrop of our favorite dramas of the will." [68]

However, when all that is said and done, we recognize that *An American Tragedy* is a deviant from the mainstream of American literature. Dreiser's modernization of

68. Robert Penn Warren, "An American Tragedy," *Yale Review*, LII (1962), 7–8.

Greek fate into scientific naturalism is so monolithic that it becomes naïve. First, Dreiser can conceive of cosmic law, but not of purpose in the naturalistic universe. Thus, he can envision suffering and pain, but no way to make it meaningful. There is relentlessness in the universe, but no equilibrium, for there is no *agon* of enough magnitude possible between fate and man as to place equilibrium even momentarily in doubt. So we have the trappings of Greek tragedies of fate, but not their consequences. The catharsis that is engendered by Dreiser's tragic vision is one of terror, but of a rather detached sort. He denies us the deepening of terror that comes of individuated identification with the tragic hero. As John Von Szeliski said, Dreiser's "philosophy of irresponsibility" led him into a concept of tragedy "where man is tragic because he is born; because he cannot control his destiny by will and talent." [69] In other words, the tragic world of *An American Tragedy* does not admit a tragic tyrannos.

In his biography of Dreiser, F. O. Matthiessen refers to Melville's *Pierre* and remarks that in a story of a young character completely "dominated by fate ... we do not have the catharsis that can come only out of some mature struggle against doom." [70] Dreiser's conception of tragedy in *An American Tragedy* does not envision Emerson's antidote to the enervation of ostensible fate—the active hero. Clyde has a dull mind, selfish and infantile. His is "a weak and scattered mind ... never able to face the real facts," Matthiessen says. "He shows no trace of greater maturity." [71] With-

69. Von Szeliski, "Dreiser's Experiment," 32–33. See Robert Shafer's brief comparison of *An American Tragedy* with the *Oresteia* of Aeschylus in "*An American Tragedy*: A Humanistic Demurrer," in Alfred Kazin and Charles Shapiro (eds.), *The Stature of Theodore Dreiser* (Bloomington: Indiana University Press, 1965), 123.
70. F. O. Matthiessen, *Theodore Dreiser* (New York: William Sloane, 1951), 207.
71. *Ibid.*, 203.

out mind to stand in awe of what is expected of him, there is no anagnorisis. Without anagnorisis, the ultimate terror is still unconfronted, and pity is only superficial at best.

Much irony lies in Dreiser as a tragedian. It is the very unpalatable characteristics of his work—the heavy style, embarrassingly direct earnestness, accumulation of detail to the point where patience is overwhelmed—that led Warren to pronounce him a tragedian and Matthiessen to say that he wrote "out of a profoundly tragic sense of man's fate." [72] But we dare not mistake his profound sense of man's fate for a profound concept of it. His plot is simple: it depicts the fate of a young man caught in mechanistic naturalism, without any glimpse of purpose or morality in heaven or on earth. His hero's adventures and his hero's nature are so simple as to preclude the development of tragic paradox. Without an ostensible belief in meaning and value, Dreiser cannot depict meaning and value. No tragedy can arise in such a fiction.

The third of the Greek progeny in American tragedy, Maxwell Anderson's *Winterset* (1935), is a particularly derivative play. Shakespeare, for example, contributed *Hamlet* for revenge motif; *Romeo and Juliet* for the star-crossed love between Mio and Mariamne; *Lear* for the character of Judge Gaunt and the Hobo-Fool; and *The Tempest* for elements of the characterization of Esdras. Yet these are relatively superficial influences. Of greater significance are the themes of tragic fate and of the tragic quest for knowledge that Anderson got from the Greeks (after a glance or two at the Book of Job).

After two costume tragedies of overly familiar heroines, *Elizabeth the Queen* (1930) and *Mary of Scotland* (1933), *Winterset* attempts to be tragedy of Anderson's own time. The plot of *Winterset* arises out of an event that rocked the

72. *Ibid.*, 207.

foundations of American society—the miscarriage of justice called the Sacco-Vanzetti affair. In the seismographic importance of the case, Anderson saw not only social shock waves, but also trepidations of cosmic magnitude. Anderson was aware of the problem of magnitude in modern realistic theater and tried in several ways to push the plot of *Winterset* beyond its commonplace confines to the thematic arena of Greek tragedy. In the first place, he wrote it in verse. For poetry traditionally was reserved the stuff of universality and eternality, and, Anderson implies, by itself has a quality of largeness that aggrandizes even an everyday event. He wrote: "*Winterset* is largely in verse, and treats a contemporary tragic theme, which makes it more of an experiment than I could wish, for the great masters themselves never tried to make tragic poetry out of the stuff of their own times." [73] Mio and others in *Winterset* speak in meters. It is also noteworthy that Ahab speaks sometimes in a blank verse prose, and startling metaphors dot the speech of Lavinia Mannon, Willy Loman, and Blanche DuBois. Poetry in the mouths of such may not, of course, be great verse, but neither does it degrade them. Poetry in American drama, Anderson predicted, will transcend the "journalistic" in our lives, that is, the immediacy of our political, social, and economic existence, and will use these commonplace blocks of life to build a "cathedral [which] house[s] the mysteries." [74] Actually, poetry never got that far in American theater, but Anderson reaches for this sublimity in *Winterset*.

With this stylistic hint that more is involved in this version of Sacco-Vanzetti than merely contemporaneous headlines, Anderson develops the aura of magnitude by fashioning a hero with pretensions of being a tyrannos. He

73. Maxwell Anderson, "A Prelude to Poetry in the Theatre," intro. to *Winterset* (Washington, D.C., 1935), xi.
74. *Ibid.*, viii.

purports at least a sense of destiny, and his speech, and that
of certain characters surrounding him, contains intermittent allusions to larger-than-life literature of the past, thus
seasoning the play with a certain portentousness that promises magnitude. Anderson's hero is the son of one of the un-
justly convicted men. But this boy, Mio Romagna, is not his
own man: he is a product of the curse upon his family, of his
own nature, and of the immutable machinations of some
force beyond society. Therein lies the Greek impulsion, and
even in our socioeconomic naturalistic epoch, that vision
is wondrous indeed. Once again, it is the ancient mystery of
the chosen individual, born with the appropriate personality that will not permit him (in Arthur Miller's words)
"to walk away," who is thrust into an *agon* fashioned by the
external power. Mio's good friend, Carr (his Horatio) asks:

> ... You have to try?
> MIO: Yes.
>   Yes. It won't let me alone. I've tried
>   to live and forget it—but I was birthmarked
>   with hot iron into the entrails.[75]

The ineluctable call to his inner nature (reflecting Job),
indeed to his prenatally determined destiny (recalling Oedipus), is accompanied by a grand old plot out of *Hamlet*,
ultimately harking back to O'Neill's favorite myth, the
Oresteia. The commingling of a feel of destiny with prior
knowledge of stories of tragedy adds weight to the story of
Mio Romagna, a son badgered by conscience and pride, who
comes to avenge the father.

> MIO [to Carr]: This thing didn't happen to you.
>   They've left you your name
>   and whatever place you can take. For my heritage
>   they've left me one thing only and that's to be

75. *Winterset*, in Maxwell Anderson, *Four Verse Plays* (New York: Harcourt, Brace, 1954), Act I, 30. Each play is separately paginated. Hereafter
references to the play will be by act and page number in this edition.

my father's voice crying up out of the earth
and quicklime where they stuck him. (I, 29)

What is vitally significant to realize here is that Mio con-
fuses the societal *they*—those who committed the unjust act,
killed his father, and tampered with his name—with the
cosmic *they*—the capricious gods who have overseen evil
and injustice all the way back to the aboriginal murder of
Abel by Cain (echoed in Mio's lines; cf. Genesis 4:10: "thy
brother's blood crieth out unto me from the ground"). It
is a purposeful confusion, for thus Anderson conceives of
the long arm of fate reaching out from a racial and immediate past to tap the chosen hero on the shoulder. We have
catapulted far beyond society.

The enactment into which Mio's fate has cast him re-
hearses the archetypal search for knowledge enacted long
ago by Job and Oedipus. But Anderson does something a
little different here. Whereas the question of justice is only
a minor part of Job's question and no part of Oedipus',
Anderson equates the acquisition of truth with the fulfillment of justice. His concept of tragedy, then, is ancient,
truly as religious as he once said drama always was: the hero
serves as the community's representative, its king-priest, as
it were, and in his catastrophe the sins of the community
are to be cleansed.

In *Winterset* we perceive, as in *An American Tragedy*,
the equation of naturalism and fate, but Anderson's ad-
vocacy of this twentieth-century brand of fatalism[76] does
not preclude a belief in "God, the Fates, or some other
scheme of retributive justice [which] makes the writing of
tragedy seem a valid act." [77] Nor does Anderson invalidate

76. Robert Roby, "Two Worlds: Maxwell Anderson's *Winterset*," *College
English*, XVIII (1957), 195–96.
77. H. A. Watts, "Maxwell Anderson's Tragedy of Attrition," *College
English*, IV (1943), 221.

the tragic search for knowledge by an active hero, which is a concept of tragic heroism quite unlike Dreiser's and more Greek.

So significant is the vision of the active hero against the onslaughts of despair that Anderson wants us to know that, sometime before the play opens, Mio had considered momentarily an alternative that neither Oedipus nor Job would have considered:

> CARR: Last time I saw you, you couldn't think
> of anything you wanted to do except curse
> God and pass out. (I, 26)

This echo of the advice from Job's wife marks the nadir of Mio's mood as it occurred, significantly, before the play opens. We are to witness a characteristic American reversal of Aristotelian peripety. Mio's fortunes cannot worsen, but he gains size and nobility.

As usual, it is Oedipus Tyrannos who is the guiding exemplar. Mio displays the traits of the American tyrannos: persistence, endurance, bravery, ingenuity, and a soft heart. It is proper to thrust him into an *agon* involving a conflict with terrestrial antagonists, recognizing that his encounter is with cosmic powers. In a careful analysis of the relationship of Oedipus and Mio, J. T. McCullen has noted that both are cursed into their tragic situations by "a sense of duty to the dead" and both "achieve spiritual freedom through discovery of knowledge." [78] What this otherwise admirable analysis fails to do is to emphasize two transcendently important characteristics: first, for both heroes, the true antagonists are his friends; and second, learning the truth does not do a blessed thing for these heroes—in fact, they are damned by it.

78. J. T. McCullen, "Two Quests for Truth: *King Oedipus* and *Winterset*," *Laurel Review*, V (1965), 29.

The first of Mio's "comforters" is Esdras. Circumstances force Esdras to use his talmudic mind to rationalize why the truth should not be told, justice should not be sought, and Mio's quest should not be fulfilled. He says:

> We ask a great deal of the world
> at first—then less—and then less. We
>   ask for truth
> and justice. But this truth's a thing
>   unknown
> in the lightest smallest matter—and as for
>   justice,
> who has seen it done? (II, 71)

And so, Esdras concludes, "Those who lost . . . [will] not rise again, and their causes lie there with them." Why go on with the search? Of course, Esdras fails as old Tiresias failed with Oedipus and the comforters with Job. Mio pushes on.

Next comes his new love, Miriamne, sister of Garth, a witness to the murder for which Mio's father was executed. Cries Miriamne to Mio concerning her beloved brother:

> He's punished, Mio.
> His life's been torment to him. Let him go,
> for my sake, Mio.

His reply is:

> I wish I could, I wish I'd never seen him—or you.
> . . . I've steeped too long
> in this thing. It's in my teeth and bones. I can't
> let go or forget. And I'll not add my lie
> to the lies that cumber his ground. We live our
>   days
> in a storm of lies that drifts the truth too deep
> for path or shovel; but I've set my foot on a
>   truth
> for once, and I'll trail it down! (III, 121)

Mio is quite aware that this situation goes far beyond the casuistry of an old man prostituting his reason to protect his son, or the threat of death by a racketeer brandishing a gun, or even the love of Miriamne. The tyrannos in Mio acknowledges the power of the gods as authors of life's actions. After he finally learns that Trock is the murderer and Garth was a witness, Mio exults:

> . . . Now I could almost wish
> There was a god somewhere—I could almost think
> there was a god—and he somehow brought me here
> and set you down before me here in the rain
> where I could bring this out of you! (II, 100)

He also acknowledges the gods as mockers:

> (*Looking up*)
> Now all you silent powers
> that make the sleet and dark, and never yet
> have spoken, give us a sign, let the throw be ours
> this once on this longest night . . .
>   We are two lovers
> here in your night, and we wish to live. (III, 129)

The tiny piece of knowledge vouchsafed to Oedipus and to Mio is but symbolic of the concept of knowledge treated philosophically in Job: the human quest for knowledge is answered with a display of cosmic power. For two acts, the cosmic initiators of the action stand aside, like God in the Book of Job, and allow puny humans to roll out their destiny. When finally Mio is about to complete his destined mission, the gods bestir themselves. Mio acknowledges their governance thus:

> The gods were damned ironic
> tonight, and they've worked it out . . .
> The bright ironical gods!
> What fun they have in heaven! When a man prays
>   hard

for any gift, they give it, and then one more
to boot that makes it useless. (II, 109)

Together with Miriamne (drawn inexorably into Mio's orbit just as the wife of Job and Jocasta, wife of Oedipus, were pulled into the catastrophes of those heroes), Mio is gunned down by two silent ministers of nemesis, appropriately serge-suited.

Recalling the technique of catharsis and epilogue in Greek drama, Anderson writes a final choric ode for Esdras that expresses his naturalistic lesson: " . . . knowing not/ what the fires mean to right and left, nor whether / a meaning was intended or presumed" by fate. But Anderson is neither a Sophocles, ready to bow before the power of cosmic caprice, nor a Dreiser, ready to condemn his hero to bovine passivity. He has Esdras perceive in his heart "something dim in distance" and intone over the bodies of Mio and Miriamne the epitaph for American tyrannoi whose heroism American tragedians learned from the Greeks:

. . . Know this where you lie,
this is the glory of earth-born men and women,
not to cringe, never to yield, but standing;
take defeat implacable and defiant,
die unsubmitting. (III, 133)

A PRIDE OF SOUTHERN TYRANNOI

The scene shifts from New England to the South, from Cabot's farm and Mannon's mansion to Sutpen's Hundred, from the slums of New York to the back roads of Louisiana and the slums of New Orleans, from the heart of one mythic region to the heart of another. In *Absalom, Absalom!* and *All the King's Men*, William Faulkner and Robert Penn Warren, like O'Neill, spin tragedies of tyrannoi who made it for a moment. In *A Streetcar Named Desire*, Tennessee Williams, like Dreiser and Anderson, wrote a tragedy of a

dreamer who did not. The change of locale changes only
the life-style of the tragic hero. The necessity of the tragic
confrontation, the imposition upon his personality, the
battle against time, history, and circumstance all remain the
same. Into these heroics flow legacies from ancient and
American *tyrannoi* who grasped for permanent promises,
only to traverse the peripety to ironic death.

In *Absalom, Absalom!* (1936) Faulkner displays a democratic tragedy of magnitude that we must go back eighty
years, to *Moby-Dick*, to find again. Both are able at once to
establish the largeness of their tragic heroes and thereby,
their stories. Their portentous and mysterious Gothicism
smothers us so completely that the posturing of their heroes
takes on at once the intended aura of significance. In *Moby-
Dick*, the broad epical flow of incident, comment, and detail implies the deep significance of the action; in *Absalom,
Absalom!*, an epical sweep of the story is also effected, but
in a different way.

Thomas Sutpen looms so large that his story can be told
only from the angles of experience and conjecture of several narrators covering at least three generations. It is a
spider web of construction. Vertical strands are woven by
the narrators, who interpolate upon one another connect-
ing strands. Bit by confused bit, circuitously, repetitiously,
with convoluted backing and filling, the story is interpreted,
conjectured, evaluated, until the design is finished and the
house of Thomas Sutpen crashes in tears and flames, physical manifestations of a catharsis conjoined in by narrators,
listeners, and readers.

In the center of the web stalks the centripetal figure of
Thomas Sutpen, designing, weaving, silent, relentless, irre-
frangible, another exemplar of the fact that in American
tragedy the breadth of plot depends upon the magnitude we
are made to perceive in the protagonist. We never directly

see or hear Thomas Sutpen act or talk in *Absalom, Absalom!* He is always seen largely through the filter of someone else's vision—Rosa Coldfield, the elder Compson, Quentin Compson, and Shreve McCannon, the sensitive, perceptive outsider, who at the final stranding of the web, becomes our alter ego. From the moment Sutpen rode into Jefferson, alone and friendless, in 1833 he had whelming size: "The stranger's name went back and forth among the places of business and idleness and among the residences in steady strophe and antistrophe: Sutpen, Sutpen, Sutpen, Sutpen," (32)[79] as if already there were something Greek and mythic about him.

And biblical, as signaled by the title of the book. Faulkner's use of the Bible, as is typical in American literature, focuses upon only one aspect of a biblical story. Sutpen is never an eager, attractive youth in *Absalom, Absalom!* like David of the Bible; there is no Saul, no Jonathan, no psalm singing. More significantly, there is no Solomon who will complete the temple his father began to build. King David attracted Faulkner because he was a tyrannos who thought his cleverness and ingenuity were blessed of God so that he could found a dynasty. Was he not encouraged by the success of his exploits? Was he not saved by the hand of the Lord and vouchsafed to come to Jerusalem and establish the dynastic line as destined long before? Is not his fate clear and irrevocable? Another tyrannos, Oedipus, who with ostensible rectitude felt the same way, discovered tragically that there is more to the story than his plans and passions.

David the king fathered Amnon, the eldest son, who coveted and lay with his half sister Tamar and was later

79. William Faulkner, *Absalom, Absalom!* (New York: Modern Library, 1936). Text quoted from the novel will be from this edition, and page numbers will be in parentheses.

killed by her blood brother Absalom, who in turn rebelled against his father. David's whole vision of a dynasty built from his young loins is blotted out, smear by smear, until he finally settles in his dotage upon the young Solomon.

Here is Thomas Sutpen, who, like ancient heroes and some American ones, arises out of the common folk—his perhaps the most common, poor white trash in the hills of western Virginia. He too seems blessed of the Lord and is encouraged to envision, like Oedipus and David and Ephraim Cabot, a grand dynasty, founded on hard work, persistence, ingenuity, and the apparent blessing of the Almighty. Sutpen embodies Faulkner's conception of a tyrannos, perhaps the most complete tyrannos in American literature. And it is part of his conception that Sutpen, too, has his Amnon in Charles Bon, his Tamar in Judith, his Absalom in his son Henry.[80] Finally, the unkindest irony of all: Thomas, in his desperate middle age, tries to father a Solomon by Milly Jones (some Bathsheba, she!) and all he begets is a bastard girl and his own death. How are the mighty fallen! This is nearly classical peripety.

Sutpen is a tragic tyrannos in a region intoxicated with the memory of tragic tyranny. Sutpen is fated by a fearful determinism that flows out of the past and quagmires time. As in New England, where there is no escape from the Puritan inheritance, so the South cannot grope beyond the control of a congenital guilt arising from its religion and history.[81] It is difficult to agree with Robert Jacobs' asser-

80. Ilse D. Lind, "The Design and Meaning of *Absalom, Absalom!*" *PMLA*, LXX (1955), 888–89. My indebtedness to this article on a number of points in this chapter is not always demonstrable by exact citations, but is nevertheless great.

81. A lengthy reiteration of the place of the South in Faulkner's tragic vision is unnecessary here. See *ibid.*, 887; Cleanth Brooks, "History and the Sense of the Tragic: *Absalom, Absalom!*" in Robert Penn Warren (ed.), *Faulkner: A Collection of Critical Essays* (Englewood Cliffs, N.J.: Prentice-Hall, 1966), 197–98; and Melvin Backman, "Sutpen and the South: A Study of *Absalom, Absalom!*" *PMLA*, LXXX (1965), 596–604.

tion that the tragedy in this novel is "human" because the whites in the South made Negroness a divine fate and so "misconstrue[d] the nature of [this] fate, which is of human working, not divine." [82] The myth upon which southern consciousness is founded—at least according to Faulkner, Warren, and Williams—is as impervious to social amelioration as the myth of Apollo is to the science of astronautics, or the myth of Oedipus to psychoanalysis. It simply exists, inviolable and sanctified.

Indeed, Rosa Coldfield is astounded that God would permit His home to be the place where the Sutpen plan was to incubate, where Sutpen would meet the virginal beauty, her sister Ellen, destined to mother his dynasty: "In church, mind you [she complains to Quentin Compson], as though there were a fatality and curse on our family and God Himself were seeing to it that it was performed and discharged to the last drop and dreg. Yes fatality and curse on the South and on our family as though because some ancestor of ours had elected to establish descent in a land primed for fatality and already cursed with it . . . coerced by Heaven into establishing itself in the land and the time already cursed" (21). Quentin Compson's grandfather also perceives some kind of power up there directing the enactment. As if witnessing a Greek tragedy he sees Sutpen as "an actor 'still playing the scene to the audience, behind him Fate, destiny, retribution; irony—the stage manager, call him what you will.' " [83]

---

82. Robert D. Jacobs, "Faulkner's Tragedy of Isolation," in Louis Rubin, Jr., and Robert D. Jacobs (eds.), *Southern Renascence: The Literature of the Modern South* (Baltimore: The Johns Hopkins University Press, 1953), 173, 179, 191.

83. This passage is quoted by Jacobs, *ibid.*, to support his contention that old man Compson is a "purveyor of spiritless and jaded determinism" based on a notion of "outmoded Fate" and of an "omnipotent Jester." However, *Light in August* contains an analogous image of the Player and His chess game (New York: Modern Library, 1950), 405–407. Since in that novel Faulkner speaks in his auctorial authority, we may assume this image constitutes part of his cosmic vision.

It is Shreve McCannon, a Canadian boy, who perceives the syndrome of time and history as surrogate deific powers:

> We [Canadians] don't live among defeated grandfathers and freed slaves . . . and bullets in the dining room table and such, to be always reminding us never to forget. What is it? Something you live and breathe in like air? a kind of vacuum filled with wraithlike and indomitable anger and pride and glory at and in happenings that occurred and ceased fifty years ago? a kind of entailed birthright father and son and father and son of never forgiving General Sherman, so that forevermore as long as your children's children produce children you won't be anything but a descendant of a long line of colonels killed in Pickett's charge at Manassas?
> "Gettysburg," Quentin said. "You can't understand it. You would have to be born there!" (361)

Quentin is wrong, of course. Readers anytime can well understand and approximate the pity and terror felt by a southern boy in 1910, just as we spiritually join the pagans of Athens of two millennia ago in their anagnorisis and catharsis at the end of their tragedies. Clearly, Faulkner's concept of tragedy is as universal as every other tragedian's, and he makes his hero transcend his contemporaneous moment and geographic spot to reach archetypal stature. For it is the age-old confrontation of innocence and guilt without sin, of man and fate, that he intends to portray, and to that end, the South is but a pasteboard mask to be cut through to get at the truth.

For this confrontation, Faulkner fashions a tyrannos with so gigantic a dose of proper Greek hubris that he at once represents the grandiose American myth of rags to riches and soars beyond it. Arthur Schlesinger, Sr., once described the national myth as the "conviction that nothing in the world is beyond [the American's] power to accomplish." [84] In Faulkner's tragic world the gods who pay attention to

84. Quoted by Brooks, "History and the Sense of the Tragic," 193.

American democratic tyrannoi choose their protagonist because he has the hubris they love to play with. Then they
hoist the hero on his own petard of heroism. Therefore,
Faulkner fashions his hero with the characteristics of the
genealogy of grandeur continuous from Prometheus to Lavinia Mannon and evolves his tragedy with the bitter theme
of innocence outraged by irony.

Quentin Compson recalls that "[Grandfather] said how
Sutpen was talking about it again, telling him again . . .
how he thought there was something about a man's destiny
(or about the man) that caused the destiny to shape itself to
him like his clothes did" and goes on to comment, "so . . .
his . . . destiny had fitted itself to him, to his innocence, his
pristine attitude for platform drama and childlike heroic
simplicity" (245–46). Again, the proud innocent is arbitrarily chosen, because his nature is proud and innocent:

> Sutpen's trouble was innocence [Quentin explains to Shreve].
> All of a sudden he discovered, not what he wanted to do but
> what he just had to do, had to do it whether he wanted to or
> not, because if he did not do it he knew that he could never
> live with himself for the rest of his life, never live with what
> all the men and women that had died to make him had left
> inside of him for him to pass on, with all the dead ones wait-
> ing and watching to see if he was going to do it right, fix
> things right so that he would be able to look in the face not
> only the old dead ones but all the living ones that would
> come after him when he would be one of the dead. (220)

This characteristic of innocence that Faulkner clothes
his hero with has several important aspects that aid the
coming catharsis, and every one of them is intertwined with
the onslaught of irony. The hubris in Sutpen makes him a
grotesque, a demon (as Rosa Coldfield and Shreve McCannon call him), a victim of his own obsession of dynastic design, and a symbol of guilt; the innocence in him saves him

from a judgment of villainy and evil. He suffers from the tragic metastasis of virtue, a condition that always afflicted tragic heroes with what Melville called the "madness of vital truth." This Faulkner makes Rosa perceive, even she who is so antipathetic to Thomas Sutpen: "If he was mad, it was only his compelling dream which was insane and not his methods. . . . I . . . did believe there was that spark, that crumb in madness which is divine, though madness knew of no word itself for the terror or pity" (166–67).

These paradoxes are but the first irony of innocence, the one which feeds the growing sense of terror in the reader. The others feed the balancing sense of pity. The hubris that made Sutpen magnificent is whittled down to size by an innocence that makes him finite. His virtues become blinders to any awareness of his own responsibility for the despair of his son Henry, the death of Charles, and the stoic resignation of Judith. We begin to pity because Sutpen is demeaned by a bafflement so complete that he does not know he is baffled. His sense of destiny magnifies the pitiful absurdity of his proposal to Rosa Coldfield, and later of his desperate liaison with Milly Jones—a relationship so bankrupt that it parallels the vista of his decrepit mansion, burnt-out fields, and blasted dynasty.

When this tyrannos begins to lose control, our hearts refuse to lay at his hand the sins with which his children are visited. We see the once powerful tyrannos stripped to a desperate animalism, like Lear naked on the heath, scrambling to put the shattered pieces back into some kind of compromised order. In *Absalom, Absalom!*, too, is bared a "sight most pitiful." And then, as Shreve McCannon perceived, "the final outrage and affront": Wash Jones kills Sutpen with ". . . that scythe, symbolic laurel of a caesar's triumph—that rusty scythe loaned by the demon himself

to Jones more than two years ago to cut the weeds away"
(177–78).

Faulkner strategically reserves almost until the last the
most affecting moment of Sutpen's life. We have already
been told through the chronological disorder of the narrators' remembrances of his origins, his character, his rise,
his peripety, his desperation, and his death. We are in the
midst of reordering our sensibilities about this man, when
Faulkner flashes back to a night during the Civil War. Ap-
pomattox is in the offing and circumstance places Sutpen
and his two sons in the same camp for one night. The air
of defeat weighs heavily upon the bivouac south of Rich-
mond, but, though defiance is gone, stubbornness remains.
Charles Bon is asleep; Henry Sutpen is called quietly to the
tent of a visiting colonel, Thomas Sutpen. Here Faulkner
gives us a different Sutpen from the one we know—no brag-
gadocio, no calculation, no cold superiority. Here Sutpen
is a father, concerned with the news that his son had been
wounded at Shiloh: ". . . Henry is aware that he has moved,
was going to move, moved by what of close blood which in
the reflex instant abrogates and reconciles even though it
does not yet (perhaps never will) forgive, who stands now
while his father holds his face between both hands, looking at it . . . —Henry, Sutpen says—my son." (353). This is
Thomas Sutpen's last scene, Faulkner's last word on his
hero. Magically, pity for Thomas Sutpen is aroused.

Does this tragic hero suffer anagnorisis, the discovery of
the meaning of his catastrophe? Some critics claim he does
not.[85] In the novel, Rosa reports his willful refusal to accept the fact of his loss, calling, rather, upon his original
belief in his destiny: *"He talking not about me or love or*

85. *Ibid.*; Jacobs, "Faulkner's Tragedy of Isolation," 170; Lind, "The Design and Meaning of *Absalom, Absalom!*" 907.

marriage, not even about himself and to no sane mortal lis-
tening nor out of any sanity, but to the very dark forces of
fate which he had evoked and dared out of that wild brag-
gart dream where an intact Sutpen's Hundred which no
more had actual being now (and would never have again)
than it had when Ellen first heard it" (165). And Grandfather Compson testifies to his refusal to accept the moral
implications of it: "Not moral retribution you see: just an
old mistake in fact which a man of courage and shrewdness . . . could still combat if he could only find out what
the mistake had been" (267–68). Yet can a man of such consummate idealism and realism, who planned and actually
built upon such a dream, ignore the fact of its ruined condition entirely? I think not. Though I have no text to help
me, I can imagine that when Thomas Sutpen lay alongside
trash like Milly Jones, his anagnorisis was so intense and
desperate that he refused to think it aloud for somebody to
relate.

The meaning of the catastrophe grows upon the character
who serves as the reader's alter ego, Shreve McCannon.
Shreve imagines the action that took place during the gaps
in Quentin's narrative, using the clues and characters that
Quentin is able to provide. In these conjectures, we trace
the evolving awareness that leads Shreve (and us) to catharsis. Midway in the telling of the tale, Shreve shows a naïve
moral extremism when he imagines Thomas Sutpen as
"this Faustus, this demon, this Beelzebub . . . engaged in
one final frenzy of evil and harm-doing before the Creditor
overtook him next time for good and all" (178). Here the
Deity as Creditor sits passively in His countinghouse waiting to tot up Sutpen's tragic flaws. Later, Shreve reaches a
point where a growing consciousness of moral interaction
between divine plan and human circumstance, between
fate and tyrannos, begins to take seed. He imagines that

Charles Bon, hundreds of miles away, when yet a child ignorant of his father, was reared and prepared for the confrontation with the father that rejected him. " 'He is your father [he is taught]. He cast you and me aside and denied you his name. Now go,' and then set down and let God finish it: pistol or knife or rack; distinction or grief or anguish; God to call the shot or turn the wheel" (297). The Creditor has become a God who is expected to operate a mechanism of justice in any way that pleases Him, but He is still conceived of as the passive outsider. Finally, Shreve discerns in the long process of Charles Bon's education, and even in the Civil War itself, a relentless, inscrutable purposefulness of a tragic action divinely and morally authored. He conjectures that Henry wondered ". . . *maybe from that moment the whole purpose of the retreat seemed to him to be that of bringing him within reach of his father, to give his father one more chance"* (347).

So, for Faulkner, moral purpose infuses and transcends time, history, the war, the grand design, the confrontation, the myth. That moral purpose involves God's power and inscrutability. The tyrannos is killed; his vision blotted out. He deserves his catastrophe, and he creates a family curse that ends with the idiocy of a grandson and the suicide of a bedeviled young man at Harvard. The sins of the father indeed are visited upon the progeny to the third generation. It is an Old Testament God that evoked this Greek tragedy. Moral equilibrium prevails.

Absalom, Absalom! is a grand moment in the history of American tragedy. It portrays the mind and psyche of a true American tyrannos in his ironic glory and catastrophe. In the American way, it colors the inscrutability of Greek fate with the inscrutability of a trustworthy Christian God. Perhaps the ultimate fillip of pity and terror is this: poor Quentin Compson, a southern boy, cannot squirm out of the quagmire of the meaning of the South; Shreve McCannon, a Canadian, finally sees the story in all its universality and lives, as we do, enriched and cleansed by it.

A quarter century after the publication of *All the King's Men* (1946), the gigantic shadow of an actual southern tyrannos, Huey Long, still hovers over the character of Robert Penn Warren's hero, Willie Stark,[86] as if it really mattered—as if, indeed, it really matters whether Shakespeare's historiography, for example, was accurate in his portrayal of tragic heroes. It was this narrow view of Warren's creation against which Robert Heilman rightfully inveighed when he scolded the reviewers for criticizing Warren on sociological or historical grounds.[87] *All the King's Men* is a political novel, of course. But it is so only as *Oedipus* and Shakespeare's tragedies are political plays. Out of the concerns of their time, they rise to depict not a local society, but the entire society of men.

So with the story of Willie Stark. Warren's concept of the tragic hero is typically American, particularly southern, like Faulkner's, yet universal as well. Willie rises out of a community of ignorant, hopeless, superstitious, red-neck hicks of the Louisiana countryside, and in true American mythic fashion, he clambers upward from a peeling, clapboard farmhouse to a gaudy governor's mansion. Cavalierly he takes from the rich and gives (most) to the poor, but forgets not the strategically placed politician either. Willie Stark is the man for this season in the evolution of his southern society, but it is wrong to say that a different set of social conditions would have precluded the coming of this hero. Society represents not a moment of time in social his-

86. See, for example, Ladell Payne, "Willie Stark and Huey Long: Atmosphere, Myth, or Suggestion?" *American Quarterly*, XX (1968), 580–95.
87. Robert Heilman, "Melpemone as Wallflower; or, the Reading of Tragedy," *Sewanee Review*, LV (1947), 154 ff.

tory, as far as Warren is concerned, but (in Heilman's words) a "spiritual condition—the decline of tradition, the loss of an integrating force." [88]

Warren is as aware as Faulkner of the history mystique of the South. His recognition of the power of history is reflected in the novel's narrator, Jack Burden, a self-styled student of history who becomes Willie's hatchet man and disciple. In the scheme of the novel, Warren is as interested in the moral evolution of Jack Burden as in the tragedy of Willie Stark. For our purposes, Burden serves as the dramatic foil of the hero and as the Greeklike chorus casting the immediate action onto the stage of totality of time and space.

History immobilizes Jack Burden and challenges Willie Stark. As a result of working on the papers of a distant Civil War relation, Jack is willing to accept the universe as a mechanistic set of interrelationships. Cass Mastern, the subject of his researches, adulterer with his best friend's wife during the war, the cause of her shame and his friend's suicide, finally "learned [says Burden] that the world is all of one piece."

> He learned that the world is like an enormous spider web and if you touch it, however lightly, at any point, the vibration ripples to the remotest perimeter and the drowsy spider feels the tangle and is drowsy no more but springs out to fling the gossamer coils about you who have touched the web and then inject the black, numbing poison under your hide. It does not matter whether or not you meant to brush the web of things . . . there is the spider, bearded black and with his great faceted eyes glittering like mirrors in the sun, or like God's eye, and the fangs dripping. (200)[89]

88. *Ibid.*, 157.
89. Page references in parentheses are to the later edition of Robert Penn Warren, *All the King's Men* (1946; reprint, New York: Modern Library, 1953).

To Jack Burden, God is but a haughty malevolent super-insect waiting for the first step awry and then pouncing to poisonously punish and destroy. Jack sees time as an intricate pattern of unwitting connections, with responsibility resting upon a Deity that cannot be called to answer.

For Willie Stark, however, God and time are synonyms for opportunity. He speaks like a Calvinist, acts like a realist, and dreams like a romanticist. Stark is hatefully right, we feel, when he tells Jack Burden, "Man is conceived in sin and born in corruption and he passeth from the stink of the didie to the stench of the shroud" (54). He is equally right, we feel, when he says to Judge Irwin, "There ain't a thing but dirt on this green God's globe except what's under water and that's dirt, too. . . . And God-a-Mighty picked up a handful of dirt and blew on it and made you and me and George Washington and mankind blessed in faculty and apprehension. It all depends on what you do with the dirt" (50).

A long time later, when Stark is trying to convince Dr. Adam Stanton to assume directorship of the Willie Stark Hospital, he gives the idealistic doctor a lesson in practical philosophy: "Just plain, simple goodness. Well, you can't inherit that from anybody. You got to make it, Doc. If you want it. And you got to make it out of badness. Badness . . . Out of badness . . . Because there isn't anything else to make it out of" (272). Dr. Stanton, bespeaking the words of smug, conventional idealism, asks, "How do you even recognize the good?" To which Stark replies: "You make it up as you go along. . . . When your great-great grandpappy climbed down out of the tree, he didn't have any more notion of good or bad, or right or wrong, than the hoot owl that stayed up in the tree. Well, he climbed down and he began to make Good up as he went along. He made up what he needed to do business" (273).

Thus speaks a prime tyrannos. This is not theory, mind you; it is observable, tested fact. Like tyrannoi from Oedipus to Thomas Sutpen, Willie Stark came out of the wilderness and preyed upon the weaknesses of others to achieve a measure of success by his own wits. Was it wrong? Up to almost the final moment before catastrophe, all circumstances emphasize the efficacy and rightness of the realistic, tyrannical doctrine.

But Willie Stark is no mean power grubber. He is a victim of another southern disease that goes along with history—romanticism. A persistent romantic notion of perfectability impels him. We always are given the feeling that there is sincerity in his good works and that there is more idealism in his makeup than he lets on. For example, Willie will not let Gummy Larson, a shifty contractor, bid for the job of building his hospital. He feels that edifice must have the totality of purity that he dreams of so that there will be at least one spot of God's earth which will not be dirty. But Willie is maneuvered into permitting Larson to build it, and things are not quite the same after this compromise.

It is this coil of idealism which spins off two tragic qualities in this tyrannos. First, he has a sense of destiny. He looks upon himself as a savior of his people, chosen for the job of rescuing them from the moneylenders in the temple, as it were. And relentlessly he goes about fulfilling this destiny. It is significant, I think, that he tolerates the ignorant and the merely stupid, admires the pure, but has contempt for the malingerer and cheat. Secondly, he has a capacity for anagnorisis. Willie Stark is not ignorant, nor is he callous. He is a calculator, which is very different. His neo-Calvinist philosophy reveals the fact that he thinks. He has a sense of right and wrong. No matter how great and successful a tyrannos he is, he still has the idealistic young law student's dream that the world somehow might be seen along the lines that Dr. Stanton represented. The doctor's is a world Willie knows exists. In the hospital, when Jack Burden visits the critically wounded governor, who had been shot down by Adam Stanton, Stark mutters to him, "He was all right. The Doc." After a moment, he rouses himself for one last word: "It might have all been different, Jack.... You got to believe that" (425).

Why should he care what Jack Burden believes, unless, in a moment or a lifetime of anagnorisis, he doubts his own philosophy and credits the vision of a paradisial world? Thus Willie fulfills Warren's notion of the complete man: "I suppose that the ultimate unity of knowledge is in the image of himself that man creates through knowledge, the image of his destiny, the mask he stares at. This would mean that manipulative knowledge, as well as knowledge of vision, calculation as well as conception—to take Shelley's distinction—works toward the creation of that image." [90] The complete man, it would seem, is the tragic tyrannos, assassinated by the very idealism in which he believes.

If Dr. Adam Stanton was, as Jack Burden said, the man of idea, and Willie Stark the man of fact, the difference between them was that Willie—unique among the novel's dramatis personae—suffered himself to fight and scramble to become a man of idea and died in the process. This aloneness touches off yet another bond of relationship with a past tragic hero, Job. Lucy Stark, like Job's wife, was ready to give up the battle; and Adam Stanton, Judge Irwin, and even Jack Burden, like Job's friends, all mouth the conventional homilies of traditional morality in their castigation of Willie's venality. It is only Willie who insists, and maintains, and succeeds in calling God down out of heaven. The only thing that could stop Willie is what we call ironic cir-

90. Robert Penn Warren, "Knowledge and the Image of Man," *Sewanee Review*, LXVIII (1955), 187–88.

cumstances, the accident that paralyzes his son, but really is the web of God's fate utilizing the strength of its prisoner to destroy him.

Though we wish he were otherwise constituted, we pity Willie Stark. We pity the waste of his life and the thought of what might have been that he himself utters at his death. We cannot bring ourselves to discern justice in his death, as punishment for his sins. Rather, we perceive his magnitude of character that demanded so great a display of circumstance to effect equilibrium. Therein lies a terror greater than that of a mindless mechanistic universe. As Ellis Burden, Jack's putative father, a religious fanatic with frightening insights, says: "The creation of evil is therefore the index of God's glory and His power. That had to be so that the creation of good might be the index of man's glory and power. But by God's help and in His wisdom" (462–63). Touched with evil and endowed with virtuous tyranny, Willie Stark fulfilled God's tragic will.

The third tragic hero in this pride of southern tyrannoi is Tennessee Williams' Blanche DuBois. She is not typical; she is classic—a nearly perfect combination of tyrannical aspiration, idealism, failure, and dignity, all engendered by her region's history and romantic ambience. However, these heroic qualities are not always recognized by the academic critics of the play. Popular critics did perceive them.

Though produced in 1947, midcentury indeed, the frank portrayal of the power of sex in *A Streetcar Named Desire* burst shockingly enough nearly to overwhelm the tragic themes that Tennessee Williams put into his play. For two decades, learned critics treated *Streetcar* as if it were an Ibsenian drama about a forbidden subject. Beclouded by the sad nymphomania of Blanche DuBois, the vigorous, imperial virility of Stanley Kowalski, the comfortable, satiated sensuality of Stella DuBois Kowalski, and the striking rape scene that climaxes the next to last scene of the play, Herbert Muller saw sexuality as Williams' "tragic theme," and "restoration of sexual order [as] the key to salvation and peace. . . . [There is] no wider or deeper tragic import." John Von Szeliski agreed: "The only communication and comprehension is in sex and the survivors are the sexually, albeit bestially, adjusted ones." And Robert Heilman reiterates: "The sexual commonground points up a world of imperfect choices" in which Stanley represents "a coarse new order, vigorous but rude and boorish. . . . Hope lies in Stanley and Stella." [91]

Undeniably, the air crackles with the subject. Nevertheless, sex is not beautiful in *A Streetcar Named Desire*; it is but animalistically satisfying. It certainly is not the paradisial state for Blanche; sex destroys her. It is what Stella merely settles for. Sexuality does not make Stanley into a god by any means. If he represents a well-adjusted new order, then we can only conclude that either Williams has thrown up his hands in despair or is declaring that Stanley represents mere survival, and there must be more to life than such a new order.

The point is that Williams uses sexuality tragically. It looms alongside history and time as an external power, with a like capriciousness, uncontrollability, and relentless inevitability. Like Ibsen, in *Ghosts*, Williams did not interpose sex into his play for its own sake as a theme of shock or liberation from staid, artificial gentility, but as a symbol of a relentless, nemesic past, in which the sins of the father are visited upon the children in proper Old

91. Herbert J. Muller, *The Spirit of Tragedy* (1956; reprint, New York: Washington Square Press, 1965), 273; John Von Szeliski, "Tennessee Williams and the Tragedy of Sensitivity," *Western Humanities Review*, XX (1966), 207; Robert Heilman, "Tennessee Williams: Approaches to Tragedy," *Southern Review*, I (1965), 776.

Testament fashion. Williams uses sex in *A Streetcar Named Desire* as the catalyst in the tragedy of a personality broken by death, history, and her own destined psyche. We ought not to delimit his concept to the mere portrayal of maladjusted and tawdry individuals, who need mental help and don't know it. No amount of therapy can save Blanche DuBois from confronting these powerful, uncontrollable modern surrogates of the supernal beings of old. "Williams has a long reach," his fellow tragedian Arthur Miller once wrote, "and a genuinely dramatic imagination.... His greatest value, his aesthetic valor, so to speak, lies in his very evident determination to unveil and engage the widest range of causation conceivable to him." [92]

To justify this range of causation and confrontation, Williams needed an equivalent protagonist because character, not plot, is the concern of modern tragedy. Williams' choice of a Blanche DuBois to undergo the tragic enactment and the point *in medias res* with which he begins his plot present problems, but also indicate the angle of his tragic vision. From the moment she steps onto the stage, it is clear that Blanche DuBois is not a typical tyrannos. She is beyond the capability of even attempting to control and manipulate the world about her. Nonetheless, her recollections of her former world do limn in our minds a personality that once had strength to manipulate. There still rests a deal of heroism in her, echoed in her narration of the last days of Belle Reve, her ancestral plantation house:

> I, I, *I* took the blows in my face and body! All of those deaths! The long parade to the graveyard! Father, mother! Margaret, that dreadful way! So big with it, it couldn't be put in a coffin! But had to be burned like rubbish! You just came home in time for the funerals, Stella. And funerals are pretty com-

92. Arthur Miller, "The Shadow of the Gods: A Critical View of American Theatre," *Harper's Magazine*, CXVII (1958), 46.

pared to deaths. . . . You didn't dream, but I saw! *Saw! Saw!*
And now you sit there telling me with your eyes that I let the
place go! How in hell do you think all that sickness and dying
was paid for? Death is expensive, Miss Stella! . . . Yes, accuse
me! Sit there and stare at me, thinking I let the place go! *I*
let the place go? Where were *you?* In bed with your—Polack!
(i, 26–27)[93]

Coalesced into this speech by a dowdy, abused woman
are the terrible catastrophes of an entire southern civilization. Sordid though she be, she has come to represent the
social destruction that still lingers after a century as the inescapable punishment for slavery and the Civil War; the
dissolution of a tinseled gentility founded upon inhumanity; the inexplicable victimization of a class of womanhood
by a society that forced them to marry inadequately in order
to fulfill a dream forever shattered.[94]

Belle Reve symbolizes the "universal man's Dream
House . . . turned to by man for refuge but discovered to
be only an asylum for ghosts." [95] Williams' tragic vision
casts backward beyond the single generation to include the
primordial sins of the fathers. "There are thousands of
papers stretching back over hundreds of years, affecting
Belle Reve as, piece by piece, our improvident grandfa-
thers and father and uncles exchanged the land of their
epic fornications—to put it plainly!" (ii, 43). And now,
their progenital grotesques reap the harvest of their horrid
sowing, and the terror of the black void behind us is more
than a southern legacy. It is universal.

93. Tennessee Williams, *A Streetcar Named Desire* (New York: New
American Library, 1951). Passages will be cited by scene and page from
this Signet paperback edition.

94. Robert Emmet Jones, "Tennessee Williams' Early Heroines," in Hurrell (ed.), *Two Modern American Tragedies*, 112–13.

95. Carol Smith, *T. S. Eliot's Dramatic Theory and Practice* (Princeton,
N.J.: Princeton University Press, 1963), 136, n. 24, reads the symbolism of
the mansion this way. See also E. M. Jackson, *The Broken World of Tennessee Williams* (Madison: University of Wisconsin Press, 1965), 71–82.

Though, as Robert Heilman pointed out, Blanche is not a person of hubris,[96] she is a tragic protagonist, for she has the capability of anagnorisis in the very midst of her desperate and hysterical role-playing. She knows truth and reality, knows them so well that she builds bulwarks against them—pitiful ramparts of paper shades around glaring light bulbs, of cheesy old-fashioned dresses and hats, of threadbare rituals of outmoded, inappropriate gentility, of shabby subterfuges that dissolve upon the most superficial investigation.

But until the very last scene Blanche does not lose touch with reality. She is, indeed, in a constant state of self-awareness, of recognition of who she is and what she is and what her world is like and what her immediate situation treacherously holds out to her. She says to Mitch, "I don't want realism. I want magic! (*Mitch laughs*) Yes, yes, magic! I try to give that to people. I misrepresent things to them. I don't tell the truth, I tell what *ought* to be truth. And if that is sinful, then let me be damned for it! —*Don't turn the light on!*" (ix, 117). But Stanley, of course, turns all the lights on and dispels the protective shadow of Blanche's world. To which she responds to Stanley: "I know I fib a good deal. After all, a woman's charm is fifty percent illusion, but when a thing is important I tell the truth, and this is the truth: I haven't cheated my sister or you or anyone else as long as I have lived" (ii, 41).

When Stanley strips her of all her fibs, she relates the story of her marriage to the boy poet and homosexual, whose suicide she believes she caused by expressing her disgust for him. After that she tells about her descent into casual encounters of coition, chased by the protectors of public morals in each town, until she lands here in Elysian Fields, in New Orleans. Obviously she recognizes truth,

96. Heilman, "Tennessee Williams," 781. See also Brooks Atkinson, " 'Streetcar' Tragedy," New York *Times*, December 14, 1947, Sec. 2, p. 2.

and the truth is that her life is compounded of fate and individual error and fear. Brooks Atkinson complimented the actress who created the role in New York, Jessica Tandy, by saying that she captured the essence and the nuances that Williams wrote into the role: "the terror, the bogus refinement, the intellectual alertness and the madness." [97] It's the intellectual alertness of the frustrated tyrannos that becomes the madness of vital truth which Herman Melville had seen in the dark characters of Shakespeare.

Not the least among the terrors that Blanche perceives looms the inevitability that Stanley Kowalski will be the instrument of her final catastrophe. In the famous *pas de deux* in Scene x, Stanley growls to the limp Blanche, "Tiger—tiger! Drop the bottle-top! Drop it! We've had this date with each other from the beginning!" (x, 130). It was reported that the men in the audience chortled with masculine superiority, no doubt knowing full well how successful a rationalization that claim has been since caveman days. In *Streetcar*, Stanley's boast climaxes a relentlessness that preyed upon the supersensitive nerves of Blanche from the start. As early as Scene iii, in a stage direction, she anticipates the sexual collision between her and Stanley: "*(Stanley jumps up and, crossing to the radio, turns it off. He stops short at the sight of Blanche in the chair. She returns his look without flinching. Then he sits again at the poker table.)*" (iii, 51).

Abrasion by abrasion, they come closer and closer, and Blanche with mixed despair and resignation cries out to Mitch: "He [Stanley] hates me. Or why would he insult me? The first time I laid eyes on him I thought to myself, that man is my executioner! That man will destroy me, unless . . ." (vi, 93). There is no "unless." Blanche is right. Stanley does become her executioner. He applies the *coup*

97. Atkinson, " 'Streetcar' Tragedy," 2.

de grâce to her psyche. If sex represents the old-time power
of the Greek gods, then Stanley represents a perverse *deus
ex machina,* the final piece of machinery that produces,
rather than resolves, the catastrophe. All that is left here is
the preservation of dignity, amidst the shards of the hero's
life and self, an ironic dignity devised from the anagnorisis
of the self's limitations and the power of the Other.

As part of his attempt to equalize the stature of his protagonist with the magnitude of the *agon* into which he has
thrust her, Williams makes Blanche symbolic of a world
of "thought and conscience [and] a broader humanity." [98]
She says to Stella:

> Maybe we are a long way from being made in God's image,
> but Stella—my sister—there has been *some* progress since
> then! Such things as art—as poetry and music—such kinds of
> new light have come into the world since then! In some kinds
> of people some tenderer feelings have had some little begin-
> ning! That we have got to make *grow*! And *cling* to, and hold
> as our flag! In this dark march toward whatever it is we're
> approaching. . . . [Williams' ellipsis] *Don't—don't hang back
> with the brutes!* (iv, 72)

The chief brute is, of course, Stanley Kowalski. He is, in
Harold Clurman's startling allusion, "the unwitting anti-
Christ of our time." [99]

Stanley represents that anti-force in the universe that was
long ago recognized as the partner of heroism in the tragic
enactment. He is the instrument by which the denouement
achieves catharsis. Elia Kazan, the play's director on Broadway said: "The audience at the beginning should . . . want
Stanley to tell [Blanche] off. He does. He exposes her and
then gradually, as they see how genuinely in pain, how actually desperate she is . . . they begin . . . to realize that they

98. Harold Clurman, "Review of *A Streetcar Named Desire,*" in Hurrell
(ed.), *Two Modern American Tragedies,* 95.
99. *Ibid.*

are sitting in at the death of something extraordinary . . . and then they feel the tragedy." [100]

Even Stanley finally feels some pity, some sense of guilt balanced by a sense of necessity. He remains ever the realist, but a bit of the harshness is gone. At the very least, he tries to console the distraught Stella, rather than to bellow her into submission. Hope for a new order, if any, rises not from his sexuality, but from the dim realization that he was the cause for destroying something higher than himself.

Through her defeat, asserts W. David Seevers, Williams, "the dramatist, like the psychoanalyst, makes it possible for others to be purged of guilt and fear." [101] As she walks off, on the arm of the doctor from the sanatorium, madly regal and dignified, she intones the most heartrending last line since Billy Budd's: "Whoever you are—I have always depended on the kindness of strangers" (xi, 142). The line rankles with irony, for no stranger that we have seen or heard of in this drama ever did fulfill that trust. The audience experiences a strangely counterpointed catharsis, attested to by Brooks Atkinson: "They come away from it profoundly moved and also in some curious way elated." [102]

And so, in plot, perception, and characterization, the South joins New England as the arena of tragedy. Giants stalked its earth. Though its heroes do not have royal blood, they have the royal manner, befitting the civilization that died in 1865 but left its genes to the future. One type of American tyrannos is left to discuss: the schemer who does not even have the royal manner. To the most famous example of that type we now turn.

100. Quoted in Jackson, *The Broken World of Tennessee Williams*, interpage between 84 and 85.
101. W. David Seevers, "Tennessee Williams and Arthur Miller," in Hurrell (ed.), *Two Modern American Tragedies*, 141.
102. Atkinson, " 'Streetcar' Tragedy," 2.

WILLY TYRANNOS

Ever since Arthur Miller's *Death of a Salesman* opened to Broadway success in 1949 and after it has been revived effectively on stage, screen, and television, controversy has raged over its stature as a tragedy. For many, the play is simply not a tragedy at all, because its hero, Willy Loman, cast as a type of tyrannos, is too commonplace and limited, its atmosphere is too dependent upon the delusions and weaknesses of an American materialistic society, and its problem is too ignoble for the arousal of total catharsis. Since it does not pit the hero against irresistible universal forces, it is but a fine, if pretentious, play of social protest, according to Joseph Wood Krutch.[103] A distinguished array of critics joins Krutch on this side of the argument— Richard Foster, Eleanor Clark, George Jean Nathan, William McCollom, Elder Olson, Herbert Muller. The latter's estimate is typical: *Salesman* merely tells the story of "a little man succumbing to his environment, rather than a great man destroyed through his greatness. . . . There is no question of grandeur in such a tragedy. . . . The hero may excite pity, but nothing like awe." But, judicious as always, Muller does go on to equilibrate the matter: *Salesman* is a "different kind of tragedy . . . characteristically modern," but it is a work of "uncertain intention" and less than universal in its achievement of catharsis.[104]

On the other side John Gassner, Eric Bentley, and Willy's creator, Arthur Miller, man the critical ramparts. In their animadversions on the remonstrances of the anti-*Salesman*

103. Joseph Wood Krutch, "Why O'Neill's Star Is Rising," *New York Times Magazine*, March 19, 1961, p. 108.
104. The essays by Richard J. Foster, Eleanor Clark, and George Jean Nathan are in Hurrell (ed.), *Two Modern American Tragedies*. See also William C. McCollom, *Tragedy* (New York: Macmillan, n.d.), 16–17; Elder Olson, *Tragedy and the Theory of Drama* (Detroit: Wayne State University Press, 1961), 249–50; Muller, *Spirit of Tragedy*, 272.

critics, they were not reluctant to insist that total catharsis can arise from the tragedy of a Willy Loman, or to speak of him in the same breath with untouchable heroes of yesteryear, or even to compare him with the archetype himself, Oedipus. "The common man is as apt a subject for tragedy in its highest sense as kings were," [105] declared Miller, and placed him alongside the Greek heroes and Job. In the same vein, Gassner asserted:

> I fail to comprehend why a character's failure to measure up to the "stature" of Hamlet or Lear must be a deterrent to "pity" and "fear." The case of Willy Loman in the successful production of *Death of a Salesman* would disprove this assumption. It is precisely because Willy was a common man that American audiences felt *pity* for him and *feared* for themselves. Willy was a sort of suburban Everyman with whom audiences readily established a connection, if not indeed an actual identification.[106]

The universality of the catharsis is testified to by Eric Bentley: "We all find that we are Willy, and Willy is us; we live and die together; but when Willy falls never to rise again, we go home feeling purged of (or by) pity and terror." [107]

Underlying the controversy, then, is a familiar challenge for democratic tragedy that for the Greeks was a foregone habit: magnitude of plot and character. Though Miller pooh-poohs the traditions of tragedy ("I had not understood that these matters are measured by Greco-Elizabethan paragraphs"),[108] his dramaturgical instinct forced him to agree with them on this point of magnitude. However, "if society alone is responsible for the cramping of our lives," wrote Miller, "then the protagonist must needs be so pure

105. Miller, "Tragedy and the Common Man," 171.
106. John Gassner, "Tragedy in the Modern Theatre," *Theatre in Our Times* (New York: Crown, 1954), 64.
107. Eric Bentley, "Better than Europe?" in Hurrell (ed.), *Two Modern American Tragedies*, 132.
108. Miller, *Collected Plays*, 31.

and faultless as to force us to deny his validity as a character. From neither of these views can tragedy derive, simply because neither represents a balanced concept of life." [109] Society must be seen as having more magnitude than that: " 'Society' is a power and a mystery of custom and inside the man and surrounding him." [110] In the confrontation of the individual and society, one can discern the ancient *agon* of the external power's tendency toward determinism and the hero's response to the imposition. One begins to see, then, why so many critics, and Miller himself in his introduction to his *Collected Plays*, perceive a relationship between the Greek tyrannos, Oedipus, and the American Everyman, Willy Loman.

The social frame of limitation of Willy's world does not restrict the drama to a commonplace or materialistic plot, because in his bumbling, inarticulate way, Willy Loman personifies his creator's concept that even the commonplace hero has "the human passion to surpass his given bounds, the fanatic insistence upon [his] self-conceived goal." [111] Though Oedipus' search for the truth is a conscious exercise of a powerful regal mind dealing with a problem of broad dimension and import, and Willy's quest for the truth is restrained by commonness of mind and a restricted sphere of life, yet Gassner perceives that "Willy pursues the 'truth' and struggles against it within his personal and social limits no less arduously and catastrophically than Oedipus." [112] In the generations between these two heroes, the family bloodline may have thinned a bit, but the lineaments of the tyrannos have not been elided.

It is not what society demands that makes the action, it is what Willy *thinks* it demands, and that is the unprevent-

109. Miller, "Tragedy and the Common Man," 3.
110. Miller, *Collected Plays*, 30.   111. *Ibid.*, 33.
112. Gassner, "Tragic Perspectives," 26.

able element that is the all-powerful motivation of his tragedy, as it was for Oedipus in his situation. It would seem,
then, that Miller's vision of tragedy is as broad as his prede-
cessors'. It is not society that is the primary flaw, but man's
innate, eternal, inevitable tendency to self-delusion, ironically induced by uncontrollable external powers.

This commonalty of virtuous, ironic grotesquerie relates
the king of Thebes to the Brooklyn salesman, the great intellect to the plodding huckster, the toy of the gods to the
discarded drummer. It is worth reading what Thomas Lask
perceived in this relationship:

> Certainly it is not easy to see in Willy the lineaments of an
> Othello or Oedipus. Intolerable in real life, he is almost so
> on the stage. Coarse, vulgar, banal, self-deluding, full of stu-
> pid pride, intellectually hollow, his mind is a compendium of
> yesterday's tabloid editorials. He seems scarcely the stuff of
> tragedy.
>
> Yet, to my mind, Willy represents all those who are trapped
> by false values, but who are so far on in life, that they do not
> know how to escape them. They are men on wrong track and
> know it. They are among those who, when young, felt they
> could move mountains and now do not even see those
> mountains.
>
> Aristotle said the tragic hero must be neither all good nor
> all evil, but rather a median figure. Everything about him is
> paltry except his battle to understand and escape from the pit
> he has dug for himself. In this battle he achieves a measure
> of greatness. In the waste of his life, his fate touches us all.[113]

Just so far extends Miller's depiction of a tyrannos and of
a concept of tragic magnitude. Perhaps no other American
tragedian needs so badly the perspective-righting insight of
Aristotle when he said of Euripides that though he may not
have managed the subject well, yet he was so effective that

113. Thomas Lask, "How Do You Like Willy Loman?" New York *Times*,
January 30, 1966, Sec. 2, p. 23.

he "is felt to be the most tragic of poets" (*Poetics*, Chapter 13).

Just as Miller had to narrow the cosmic proportions of a tragedy of a tyrannos to fit a democratic literature, so he had to revise the pattern of his drama. Unlike Aristotelian peripety, Willy Loman's wheel of fortune had already turned downward for him when the play opens. Willy is over the hill; his peripety is nearly complete. Material success is past; the faith in himself that had sustained him in the past has flagged badly; the hope of greatness in the name of "Loman" is now, as Biff tells his father, but the dream of a desperate, unhinged mind. The rest of the play is the fearful spectacle of watching the underpinnings of his already broken world shatter one by one. What is left for the peripety to show is the disintegration of the hero's psyche.

The method that Miller uses we have, in certain ways, already examined in other tragedies. It is the use of the past to explain the circumstances and the catastrophe of the present. The past in *Salesman* is as destructive an imposition as in New England and southern tragedies. Willy was the one who had opened up the whole New England territory. He could always sell Hartford and Boston. We witness the enactment of a memory when this was true. Speaking to the young Biff and Happy, Willy of yesterday crows, "I thank Almighty God you're both built like Adonises. Because the man who makes an appearance in the business world, the man who creates personal interest, is the man who gets ahead. Be liked and you will never want. You take me, for instance. I never wait in line to see a buyer. 'Willy Loman is here!' That's all they have to know, and I go right through" (I, 146).[114] Today, Willy of the present, with

114. The text of the play used here is the one in Miller's *Collected Plays.* Both act and page number are cited in parentheses.

what is left of his innate pride of salesmanship, says to Linda, his wife, "Oh, I'll knock 'em dead next week. I'll go to Hartford. I'm very well liked in Hartford" (I, 148). But with an inexorable sense of realization stealing over him, he verbalizes the growing doubt about himself in this very same piece of dialogue: "You know, the trouble is, Linda, people don't seem to take to me . . . I'm fat. I'm very—foolish to look at, Linda" (I, 148). Pity and terror begin to grow in the audience, who witness the torture of speaking an inner truth pushed down away from consciousness because of the very pain of it.

Right along with the torture of self-doubt and self-analysis the old Loman pride still persists. When someone calls him a walrus, he reports to Linda, he smacked him across the face. "I won't take that. I simply will not take that." But again, vacillating in pain and doubt, he admits to her, "They do laugh at me. I know that" (I, 149). There is a residue of strength in this suffering, bewildered character who has lost his way between past and present, between what he thought was good and valuable and is now turning to ashes in his mouth. Anguish and suffering are interspersed with flashes of the tyrannos.

The spectacle of self-doubt in the very grip of pride carries over to Willy's remembrance of things past, the symbols of the time when he was able to form his own world. These objects are his automobile, his house, and his son Biff. With Sophoclean irony, Miller uses the very emblems of success to symbolize the tragedy that is evolving.

The automobile is his society's symbol of Willy's profession and affluence. There are recollections of the beautiful big car that is an adventure and a ritual to polish, and the rite represented the togetherness of the self-made man and his stalwart sons (I, 143). But now the automobile has been transformed into a past memory which sharpens present pain. His New England car trip at the beginning of the play is truncated in Yonkers because the car "kept going off onto the shoulder," Willy reports to Linda. She desperately suggests that the mechanic doesn't know the car and didn't repair it properly. Willy replies, "No, it's me, it's me. Suddenly I realize I'm goin' sixty miles an hour and I don't remember the last five minutes. I'm—I can't seem to—keep my mind on it" (I, 132). Troubled by his loss of control over the car and all that it stands for in his life, he cries to his sons: "For Christ's sake, I couldn't get past Yonkers today! Where are you guys, where are you? The woods are burning! I can't drive a car!" (I, 152). Arthur Miller reports that in part *Death of a Salesman* "grew from images of futility—the cavernous Sunday afternoons polishing the car. Where is that car now?" [115]

Here is the house that Willy built. The stage directions introducing the first act describe it thus: *"An air of the dream clings to the place, a dream rising out of reality"* (I, 130). The sweet dream had once been realized, when the house had been located in a rustic section of Brooklyn. But now the neighborhood has been given over to tenement buildings, and there is hardly a piece of ground to grow a flower, and you have to crane your neck to see a star. Worst of all, the house is the scena before which is enacted the denuding of expectations. "Figure it out," Willy says. "Work a lifetime to pay off a house, you finally own it, and there is nobody to live in it" (I, 133). Of course, the "nobody" is Biff, his son. So the house comes through as the external manifestation of Willy's dream of the future, a successful Biff Loman, scion of the house of Loman. But Willy, in his own sphere, has misread the future of his house, quite like those other tyrannoi, the owner of Cabot's farm and the squire of Sutpen's Hundred.

115. Miller, *Collected Plays*, 29.

For Willy, the pride, the disappointment, the suffering are never so deeply felt, or so variously, as in relation to Biff, the almost tangible clay that Willy, tyrannos in his own house, had hoped to mold in his own image. Biff embodied, Miller wrote, "a need to leave a thumbprint somewhere in the world. A need for immortality, and by admitting it, the knowing that one has carefully inscribed one's name on a cake of ice on a hot July day." [116] We come to recognize, together with John Gassner, the heroism of this battered man's "refusal to surrender all expectations of triumph for, and through, his son. . . . Unwilling to resign to failure," Willy persists in pushing until there dawns upon him the "truth about himself and his situation." [117] Anagnorisis, in other words.

Realism demanded of Miller a concept of anagnorisis that he admittedly extrapolated from Ibsen's legacy to "forge a play upon a factual bedrock"; that is, not upon what people felt (or say they felt), but upon what they did.[118] In this light we must reinvestigate one of the most serious charges leveled at *Salesman*, that its hero is incapable of anagnorisis. For example, Joseph A. Hynes, using quoted words from a Miller essay, remarked, "For Willy Loman 'victory' would have been realization not only of Biff's love for him, but of 'who he was.' But such a 'victory' Willy could not possibly have, simply because he was created 'incapable of grappling with a much superior force'—whether Biff's love or his own dream, the two forces which 'his witlessness, his insensitivity,' and his love for Biff prevent his seeing sanely." [119] It is to Miller's credit that he

116. *Ibid.*
117. Gassner, "Tragic Perspectives," 26.
118. Miller, *Collected Plays*, 19.
119. Joseph A. Hynes, " 'Attention Must be Paid. . . ,' " in Gerald Weales (ed.), *Death of a Salesman: Text and Criticism* (New York: Viking, 1967), 286.

turns Willy's witlessness and insensitivity into means that tease the audience into an eventual anagnorisis together with the protagonist and then into a burst of pity and awe.

Willy will not let go of the echoes, and we reminisce together with him about the halcyon days. Willy recalls the glory when Biff Loman was "like a young god. Hercules— something like that. And the sun all around him. Remember how he waved to me? Right up from the field, with the representatives of three colleges standing by? And the buyers I brought, and the cheers when he came out—Loman, Loman, Loman, God Almighty, he'll be great yet. A star like that, magnificent, can never really fade away" (I, 171). But the dream is fading, rapidly and sadly. It is a kind of David-and-Absalom reenactment going on before us, of an indulgent father who cannot understand how his indulgence engenders ingratitude, disrespect, and failure in his son.

Hence, as Thomas Lask said, the bullying, the ragging, and the coarseness against those who persist in seeing the truth of it all, that dreams are but dreams and that life has a way of playing with you and not you with it. The coarseness is but the sign of the bewildered tyrannos. Willy calls Biff "a lazy bum," but a few lines later insists "Biff is not lazy" (I, 135), and then taunts him and his brother Happy with their whoring and their fancy cars (I, 152); and in his extremity extends his desperate arrogance even to Linda, to the point that Biff complains that his father wipes the floor with her (I, 162). Yet, in the hands of Arthur Miller, none of this alienates the audience; rather, it conjoins us with the protagonist. Linda herself expresses for us the sympathy we feel for the cracking protagonist: "He's not the finest character who ever lived," she cries to her sons, "but he's a human being and a terrible thing is happening to him. So attention must be paid. He's not to be allowed to

fall into his grave like an old dog. Attention, attention
must be finally paid to such a person" (I, 162).

When Biff can no longer take the bullying and what he
believes to be the pipe dreams of his father, he bursts out,
"I never got anywhere because you blew me so full of hot
air I could never stand taking orders from anybody! That's
whose fault it is" (II, 216). This is not a petulant shift of
responsibility, for we must admit Biff is right. Biff is the
crowning creature of the father-tyrannos, and this apex of
a self-created edifice of the future becomes the instrument
whereby Willy is hurtled to his anagnorisis. The conflict
between Willy and his son rises in a crescendo of traded
recriminations until Biff forces his father to face up to the
reality about both of them:

> BIFF: Pop! I'm a dime a dozen, and so are you!
> WILLY (*turning on him in an uncontrolled outburst*): I am
> not a dime a dozen! I am Willy Loman, and you are Biff
> Loman!
>
> .   .   .   .
>
> BIFF: I am not a leader of men, Willy, and neither are you.
> You were never anything but a hardworking drummer who
> landed in the ash can like the rest of them! I'm one dollar
> an hour, Willy! . . . I'm not bringing home any prizes any
> more, and you're going to stop waiting for me to bring
> them home! (II, 217)

The pitch is too high for the two of them. There is a moment of suspension, and then Biff breaks down. Weeping,
Biff moves slowly offstage.

> WILLY (*after a long pause, astonished, elevated*): Isn't that—
> isn't that remarkable? Biff—he likes me! . . . He cried! Cried
> to me. (*He is choking with his love, and now cries out his
> promise*): That boy—that boy is going to be magnificent!
> (II, 218)

It would be unrealistic if a protagonist of such limitations
would quickly give up his old dreams and adjust at once to

a new perception. Thus we hear again a litany of Biff's magnificent future, but at the same time we note something new. Willy discovers that there is a greater force than even the drive for success: love. Like the first and last plays of the ancient Oedipus trilogy, these are the forces that sustain the final actions. Willy Tyrannos is about to arrive at Colonus.

Fearfully alone now, his psyche crumbling, Willy calls upon his brother Ben, who had flitted through so many of the dream sequences as the epitome of success, hurrying on to an Alaskan gold field or an African diamond mine. But Willy's last invocation of this shade is never completed. Willy waves away all the shadows and echoes that have haunted and taunted him, telling them at last to keep silent. There is a moment of stillness, in which Willy sees into the ultimate necessity. He knows what he has to do and he goes ahead and does it—in the very symbol of his success. The offstage sound is that of an automobile speeding off and crashing into eternity (II, 220). The peripety of a man's mind is concluded.

Unlike the suicide attempts reported to us earlier in the play, this last suicide try is quite different in motivation. Those came at the nadir of Willy's bewilderment and despair; they were cowardly and escapist. This one is purposeful, self-sacrificial, and epiphanic. It is the supreme act of love for his son, and Willy Loman goes to his death with the music of unheard but remembered cheers for Biff resounding in his head. Does he have the insurance money in mind? Of course he does, being Willy. But if the money contributes to the time when "that boy will be magnificent," Willy won't be around to witness it and crow about it, and he knows that, too.

Miller summarized his tragic protagonist's anagnorisis by pointing out that Willy "achieved a very powerful piece of knowledge, which is that he is loved by his son and has been embraced by him and forgiven." The process of arriving at this knowledge engenders pity. The total commitment to a mistaken way of life, which demands in recompense the total commitment of a sacrificial catastrophe, arouses the terror.

"Requiem," the last scene of *Death of a Salesman*, parallels the choric themes at the end of *Oedipus at Colonus*. Willy's influence, so tragic in life, is effectuated properly only in death. We see this final glow emanating from the tragedy of Willy Loman in the last conversation between his two sons:

> BIFF: Why don't you come with me, Happy?
> HAPPY: I'm not licked that easily. I'm staying right in this city, and I'm gonna beat this racket! (*He looks at Biff, his chin set.*) The Loman brothers!
> BIFF: I know who I am, kid.

And when Happy persists in his tyrannical dream, Biff dismisses him "with a hopeless glance" ("Requiem," 222). In life, Willy taught Biff lessons of fraudulence; in death, he teaches him lessons of truth.

The audience, too, has learned the meaning of the tragedy of this salesman, the man who selected the wrong alternative, who misinterpreted his life as a tyrannos and thereby became a tragic figure. Arthur Miller overcame the limitations of his setting, the role of society, the commonness of his hero, to awaken catharsis in us. At the end we remember Willy Loman as what Bernard Knox said of the departed Oedipus, "a spirit which lives on in power in the affairs of men after the death of the body. His tomb is to be a holy place [and] in his grave . . . he will be powerful." [120]

This is the proper epitaph of all the other American tyrannoi as well.

120. Knox, "Sophocles' Oedipus," 23.

II

✦

The Mask of Christ

Tragedy in America, in consonance with a trend of its society's intellectual history, is inspirited not only by the muses of Olympus, but by the memory of Calvary. Almost all writers of American tragedy were brought up in the Christian faith. Implanted in a Christian society, with a history of thought that is permeated by Christian dogmas, tragedians could not ignore its doctrines and personalities. Nor could they ignore the political and social heritage of the land. This permeation of the ideas of Judeo-Christianity produced a set of heroes whose tragic mask resembles predominantly the protagonist of the first and greatest Christian tragedy, Jesus Christ.

A discussion of something called Christian tragedy causes discomfort among certain critics. Its theology cannot be reconciled, it would seem, with tragic vision. As Laurence Michel points out, evil is the root of tragedy, casting its vision entirely on man's catastrophe and on his efficacy in preserving himself. Built around the figure and meaning of Christ, Christianity preaches resurrection and redemption —the defeat of evil, sin, and death. Christian vision flings itself beyond tragedy (as the theologian Reinhold Niebuhr's book is entitled). Therefore, Michel states, "there is a basic incompatability between the tragic and the Christian view. And nothing has yet come forward which can be called,

103

without cavil, both Christian and Tragedy at the same time." [1]

This point of view can probably be maintained dogmatically, and tragedy in a Christian society, like the poets in Plato's *Republic*, can be officially proscribed. On the other hand, argues J. C. Maxwell, "This by no means is to say that a tragedy *cannot* be the product of the imagination of a Christian conscious of what his own creed implies." [2]

With regard to American tragedy, Maxwell is entirely correct. A full understanding of American tragic vision must account for such obvious Christological allusions as Arthur Dimmesdale dying in a mimesis of the Crucifixion before the populace of Boston in Nathaniel Hawthorne's *The Scarlet Letter*; Billy Budd, the primordial innocent of Herman Melville's novella, hanged from a cross yardarm; and Santiago, Hemingway's old man of the sea, collapsing beneath his shouldered mast on a via dolorosa up the hill.

American tragedy, eclectically influenced by Christian doctrine, is not a set of morality plots. We shall not see catastrophe meted out to those who commit the seven deadly sins or who do not fulfill the sacraments. The sins have been compromised; the sacraments ignored. Christian tragedy in America is heterodox, descending from its ideological elitist origins in Puritan times to the political liberalism of modern America.

Ironically, however, American liberalism has almost killed tragedy. The tendency today is to obviate a concept of guilt and individual responsibility. Guilt, we are lec-

1. Laurence Michel, "The Possibility of Christian Tragedy," in Laurence Michel and Richard Sewall (eds.), *Tragedy: Modern Essays in Criticism* (Englewood Cliffs, N.J.: Prentice-Hall, 1963), 232–33 (referred to hereafter as *Modern Essays*). One obvious candidate, however, is Eliot's *Murder in the Cathedral*. On the other hand, since medieval saint's plays are not included in the genre, I shall exempt this modern saint's play.

2. J. C. Maxwell, "The Presuppositions of Tragedy," in Michel and Sewall (eds.), *Modern Essays*, 177.

tured, is what one character in MacLeish's *J. B.* (scene ix) called a "psychophenomenal situation / An illusion, a disease, a sickness." Evil, it is claimed, is external to the individual; it is not a condition of man but of an inner psyche or an outer environment for which he is not responsible. Society and subconscious are, after all, only forms of mechanism, are they not? In such a society, tragedy presumably cannot be written. Yet, American reinterpretations of the basic tenets of Christianity have preserved the writing of tragedy and its viability as an expression of modern experience.

In the main, our tragic writers reinterpreted the concepts that Randall Stewart identifies as three essentials of the faith: the omnipotence of God, the divinity of Jesus, and the doctrine of Original Sin.[3] Insights into their revisions of dogma will afford us insights into their tragic vision.

GOD RECONSIDERED

The omnipotence of God as a personal Deity was the foundation of Puritanism, America's first type of Christianity, which dominated early American intellectual history and still remains as a residual influence. This brand of Calvinism preached the dogma of total predestination. Once the battleground of liberal theology, now it is the battleground of liberal and social theory. If man is predestined—either by a deity or by his environment or by his society—then the democratic ideal of the individual fulfilling his potential is impossible to realize. The first generation of Puritans, transferring European Protestantism to the American wilderness, had felt that their convenantal creed of Grace, Church, and Body-social—entirely theocentric in thought and act—was sufficient to face all contingencies. But

3. Randall Stewart, *American Literature and Christian Doctrine* (Baton Rouge: Louisiana State University Press, 1958), 14.

America very early began to work its heretical magic upon Old World creeds. It did not take more than a generation or two for Puritan thinkers to recognize an "implicit contradiction between Calvinism and the temper of the times." [4] As early as 1657, the Calvinist divine Richard Mather reflected the growing concept of the contraction of God's absolutism. "Tell it [to the people] as soon as they shall be able to learn," declares Mather conventionally enough, "what a solemn Covenant there is between God and heaven and them whereby the Lord takes them to be his"; but he concludes this passage with the revolutionary proviso, "If it be not through their own default." [5] To conceive of man participating in his own destiny is not merely a revision of Calvinism; it admits the contraction of the Lord's absolutism.

Mather, of course, was writing about posthumous salvation or damnation. But it is not much of a leap to a notion of man contributing to his own terrestrial destiny. Indeed, already Mather's new theology can be read as a kind of Christian endorsement of Greek tragic vision that saw man involved in an *agon* with a superpowerful deity that had predestined a set of circumstances within which the hero inescapably brings catastrophe on himself. However, the covenant of grace between God and man did add a quality to the vision of tragedy that goes beyond the classical concept. Though God narrowed His omnipotence, He did so for a morally necessary purpose. Upon this point, American tragedy permits no question and no compromise.

The axiom of God's morality serves as the bridge between Calvinist New England of the seventeenth century and Deist Philadelphia where in 1790 Benjamin Franklin sum-

4. Perry Miller, *The New England Mind: From Colony to Province* (Cambridge, Mass.: Harvard University Press, 1953), 410.
5. *Ibid.*, 411.

marized the Deistic credo which became the theology of the new democracy: "One God, Creator of the Universe. That he governs it by His Providence. That he ought to be worshipped. That the most acceptable Service we render to Him is doing good to His other Children. That the soul of Man is immortal, and will be treated with Justice in another Life respecting its Conduct in this." [6] Though God's omnipotence had been lessened, American Christianity did not conceive of Him as absent or irrelevant. Nor does Franklin see Him as a benign engineer who had created a fantastic mechanism and now lets it run perpetually. God governs. Man is still in His dominion, but free enough to be rewarded or punished for acts that he commits. Thus does Franklin, who thought himself a worthy Christian, tiptoe along that thin line that tragedy in America will take.

It was left to the transcendentalist generation of Ralph Waldo Emerson to formulate the philosophy of equilibrium between the relentless optimism of natural (undogmatic) Christianity and the relentless doubt of tragic vision. Emerson in 1836 expressed the philosophy of man's essential goodness and the promise of success in his aspirations. He insisted that "the Moral law lies at the center of nature and radiates to the circumference. It is the pith and marrow of every substance, every relation, and every process." For Emerson, this moral law operated even when he wrote about "The Tragic" a few years later. Against the fear of a thoughtless, uncontrollable nature that seems antagonistic to man, Emerson called for an equilibrium arising out of the "intellect . . . and the moral sense." [7]

6. F. L. Mott and C. E. Jorgenson (eds.), *Benjamin Franklin: Representative Selections* (New York: American Book Co., 1938), 508.

7. Stephen E. Whicher (ed.), *Selections from Ralph Waldo Emerson* (Boston: Houghton, Mifflin, 1957), 39; E. W. Emerson (ed.), *Complete Works of Ralph Waldo Emerson* (12 vols.; Boston: Houghton, Mifflin, 1904), XII, 407.

Already in his own generation two tragedies, Hawthorne's *Scarlet Letter* and Melville's *Moby-Dick*, reflected Emerson's synthesis of tragedy and morality. The tonal background for all American tragedy is created. God, an invisible character, creates the circumstances for the tragic enactment, but the suffering of the hero and the ultimate catastrophe he engenders for himself are presented as moral necessities.

Summarily then, the concept of God in American tragedy has delimited His omnipotence by devolving upon man some responsibility for his destiny and by bringing God into the action after the plot has been already committed to a certain climax. But it is clearly His world and His system of morality in which these tragedies are enacted. This concept of tragedy may sound basically like Greek fatalism, but to understand American tragedy one must differentiate between the tragedy of capricious power, which is Greek, and the tragedy of moral necessity, which is Christian. This concept is not a matter of logic; it is not within the rules of justice as man conceives of justice. It is an article of faith.

THE CHRIST THAT IS TO BE

Carlos Baker observed that it is "not infrequent in modern American fiction [that] any good man and simple man is likely to show resemblances to the Savior." [8] Scripture itself suggests a humanization of this figure. Jesus was covenanted to the Lord in an untheological ministry stressing the sublimity of the individual, the poor, and the meek, the simple grandeur of life and love. These are vaunted American traits, too.

It is from this viewpoint that Franklin, having already reinterpreted God, then reinterpreted Christ. "Jesus of Naza-

8. Carlos Baker, "The Place of the Bible in American Fiction," in James Smith and A. Leland Jamison (eds.), *Religion in American Life* (4 vols.; Princeton, N.J.: Princeton University Press, 1961), II, 271.

reth," he wrote, was only a teacher of a "System of Morals," which produced, nevertheless, "[a] Religion [that was] the best the World ever saw or is likely to see." Franklin complained that over the centuries "corrupt changes" of dogma developed in that religion and then admitted to "some Doubts as to his Divinity." [9] It is an eminent sentiment for a nation constituted on the assumption that all men are created equal.

The doubts about the divinity of Jesus were trumpeted throughout New England in the next century by irrepressible transcendentalists like Emerson and Theodore Parker. In 1838, at the Harvard Divinity School no less, Emerson proclaimed that historical Christianity "has dwelt . . . with noxious exaggeration about the *person* of Jesus," and this corruption had found for a time a place "among the Puritans in England and America. . . . But their creed is passing away." What they missed in the life of Jesus was that "alone in all history, he estimated the greatness of man. One man was true to what was in you and me." [10]

Three years later, in "A Discourse on the Transient and Permanent in Christianity," Theodore Parker resoundingly echoed Emerson's concept of the man Jesus:

> He was a man, the son of Joseph and Mary, born as we are; tempted like ourselves; inspired as we may be if we will pay the price. . . . If, as some early Christians began to do, you take a heathen view, and make him a God, the Son of God in a peculiar and exclusive sense, much of that significance of his character is gone. His virtue has no merit, his life no feeling, his cross no burthen, his agony no pain. His death is an illusion, his resurrection but a show. For if he were not a man, but a god, what are all these things? [11]

9. Mott and Jorgenson (eds.), *Benjamin Franklin*, 508.
10. Whicher (ed.), *Selections from Emerson*, 105, 111, 106.
11. Theodore Parker, "A Discourse on the Transient and Permanent in Christianity," in Perry Miller (ed.), *The Transcendentalists: An Anthology* (Cambridge, Mass.: Harvard University Press, 1950), 263, 270, 275.

There is evidently but one way that Parker sees Jesus—as the tragic figure of highest humanity, separated from a "mythus" (Emerson's word) of divinity. His passion becomes the symbol of suffering, his cross the image of the weight of guiltless responsibility, his resurrection a paradigm of the spiritual (not the physical) rebirth that tragic man can aspire to.

No matter what traditional theology taught, American tragedians could not cast their vision beyond the fact of His Crucifixion. Resurrection is God's business; for man, catastrophe—redemption in defeat—is the best he can hope for. The act of the Crucifixion becomes a symbolic act; Jesus on the cross, before the multitude, surrounded by his faithful, becomes a symbolic tableau. What remains through the centuries is the moral, but mysterious, necessity for a crucifixion, though the forms of it have naturally changed. Our Christological tragic heroes are impelled toward their catastrophes like Jesus to Calvary and, like him, suffer immolation before witnesses, who presumably are somehow purified by the experience. The lumpish sailors of the *Indomitable*, the hardhearts of Boston, Santiago's friend, the boy Manolin, are the modern counterparts of the disciples and Jerusalemites of the Gospels. In these ways of human moral necessity does the figure of Jesus still exist in the *Weltanschauung* of American tragedy. He also takes on the configurations of three parallel Christs—Job, who, we have already seen, contributed to the making of the American tyrannos; Satan, who, we shall see in the next chapter, influenced the making of another type of American tragic hero; and Adam, the chief myth-protagonist of American thought.

IN ADAM'S FALL

In America, Adam was always a fallen, humanized Christ. Like Jesus, he begins his career as a divine innocent and then is condemned by the Lord to undergo tragic tests and to suffer catastrophe. The difference between the Christ archetype and the progeny is that Adam displays a greater dimension of freedom to select the choice that God wanted him to. The wrong choice, however, is the necessary one. Adam's failure is the moral necessity that God had planned in the first place, a paradox that is featured in American tragic literature.

The Adamic myth is one of America's favorites, for America saw itself as a new Adam reborn in a new Eden. The myth reached its highest expression from 1820 to 1860, roughly from the rise of transcendentalism to the shock of the Civil War. While it flourished, writes its chief interpreter, R. W. B. Lewis, "The American myth saw life and history as just beginning. It described the world as starting up again under fresh initiative, in a divinely-granted second chance for the human race, after the first chance had been disastrously fumbled in the darkening Old World." [12]

There were, however, contemporaneous voices that read the myth of the American Adam as myths ought to be read —with an undercurrent of tragedy. What we actually learn from the Bible, declared Henry James, Sr., is not a tale of mere innocence, but an educative process of death and rebirth, in cyclic progression. It is folly to speak of rebirth without the Fall, because "only the sin made possible the rebirth; and for all its tragedy, it was a necessary sin, a subject for rejoicing." [13] The necessity of sin, the necessity of evil—moralistic dogma left over from Puritan times—dare not be ignored by the eclectic idealists. On the one hand, then, the myth of the American Adam produced "the archetypal American who has timelessly sought to realize his ideal

12. R. W. B. Lewis, *The American Adam: Innocence, Tragedy, and Tradition in the Nineteenth Century* (Chicago: University of Chicago Press, 1955), 5.
13. Quoted *ibid.*, 58–59.

Eden in the new world." [14] On the other hand, "the vision of innocence stimulated a positive and original sense of tragedy. Without the illusion, we are conscious, no longer of tradition, but simply and coldly of the burden of history . . . a sense of loss." [15]

The conception of a tragic Adam was not derived solely from the Bible. One of the greatest and influential secular Christian poets, John Milton, helped transform Adam from a doctrinal figure of sin and guilt to a tragic figure. In *Paradise Lost* we follow Adam in an awesome Aristotelian peripety from his place as a divine son of God, the zenith of creation, down to a level intensely human. Writes Northrup Frye: Adam's "tragedy seems to move up to an *Augenblick* or crucial moment" when all is suspended between the possibilities of choice, and then Adam decides to "exchange a fortune of unlimited freedom for the fate involved in the consequences of the act of exchange." [16] Theologically, of course, Adam is wrong: no love should equal the love of God. Realistically—that is to say, tragically—the love of Eve overwhelms it.

Adam succumbs to temptations that Jesus, as the son of God, rejected. But this fact only emphasizes the extent of the humanization of the son of God. At the end of *Paradise Lost*, as at the end of American Christian tragedies, the peripety of succumbing to temptation, suffering, and then rising to the demands of the catastrophe becomes the measure of tragic heroism. The nature of the tragic hero is not to walk away from human responsibilities, but to fulfill them in suffering. This is the Christological vision vouchsafed at last to an apparent sinner like Arthur Dimmesdale

14. F. I. Carpenter, "The American Myth: Paradise (To Be) Regained," *PMLA*, LXXIV (December, 1959), 604.

15. Lewis, *The American Adam*, 9.

16. Northrup Frye, *Anatomy of Criticism* (1957; reprint, New York: Atheneum, 1965), 212–13.

as well as to apparent innocents like Billy Budd and Santiago.

I say apparent innocents because linking Adam to the Christian doctrine of original sin is inescapable. In America, this is especially true. The inheritance from a Puritan ancestry says that "In Adam's fall / We sinned all," in full agreement with Christianity's teaching that Original Sin refers both to "the inherent quality of the nature of man" and to the "clear recognition that [sin's] roots lie in *a* man's character" (italics mine). By bringing racial depravity down to the level of individual depravity, Christianity sees "the origin [of sin in] the human will," and thus it becomes the "personal responsibility of each man." [17] All men are created equal—equally depraved. Each man stands equal to the next—as an individual guilty and responsible. The doctrine —ironic in its democracy and perverse in its paradox—serves fittingly as a basis for tragedy in America. The tragic hero emerges as a Christian tyrannos, exercising freedom of will within his fallible state, attempting to order his fate and master his destiny with whatever imperfect tools he has. Every act of his places him in an *agon* with his moral God because he is both innocent and guilty.

The depth of the dilemma may be perceived by the standard definitions of innocence and guilt included in Laurence Michel's discussion of the possibility of Christian tragedy: "Innocence is inclusive of the urge to be free, to escape the inhibitions of morality and mutability and evil, of finiteness and contingency and competition and waste and shame; to be one's self, to fulfill one's potential, to be man par excellence, to be like God." [18] This definition cannot be adequate, for Jesus, the exemplary innocent who serves

17. F. L. Cross (ed.), *Oxford Dictionary of the Christian Church* (Oxford, 1957), 1260.
18. Michel, "The Possibility of a Christian Tragedy," 211.

as literary archetype, decided *not* to be free when, in the American view, He joined the magnetic chain of finite humanity. Only when He suffered and died did He fulfill his potential and become a man par excellence. His catastrophe, in Hawthorne's apt oxymoron of tragedy, was one of "triumphant ignominy."

"Guilt," Michel goes on, "means failure, unworthiness, defeat, collapse, being a fool, a sinner, being a part, a prisoner; death." [19] But from Adam onward, tragic literature taught otherwise. In a world where innocence is proscribed and guilt inescapable, the consequences of tragic guilt are the gateway to the achievement of man's fullest humanity. Tragedy was never "unworthy" and the catastrophe of the guilty hero was never a "defeat."

For tragedy, other definitions, especially of guilt, had to be devised. To account for the paradox of the doctrine, Max Scheler wrote of "moral or 'guilty' guilt . . . based on the *act* of choice" and "tragic or 'unguilty' guilt . . . based on the *sphere* of choice." [20] Thus, tragic guilt is divorced from the commission of sin. Tragedy does not result from man's original *sin*, but from his original *condition*. It is this condition of human nature that Tennessee Williams was talking about when he said, "Guilt is universal. I mean strong sense of guilt. If there exists any area in which a man can rise above his *moral condition, imposed upon him at birth* [my italics], and long before birth, by the nature of his breed, then I think it is only a willingness to know it, to face its existence in him, and I think that, at least below the conscious level, we all face it." [21] Williams speaks not of sin resulting in guilt, but of a prevalent guilt without sin, demanding, nonetheless, recompense in the form of catastrophe.

19. *Ibid.*, 212.   20. Quoted *ibid.*, 225.
21. New York *Times*, March 8, 1959, Sec. 2, p. 1.

What American tragedy did with this Christian paradox may be discerned in the way catastrophe and catharsis in our genre differ from the equivalents in Greek tragedy. Aristotle reported that the most effective tragic plots were those that included the devices of anagnorisis (the scene of discovery) and suffering (the scene of pain). To the Greeks these aids to catharsis were merely a matter of plot and spectacle. Oedipus does not exhibit suffering until the scene of self-recognition and self-mutilation, nor do Hippolytus and Antigone until the death scenes. In American tragedy both effects are cast on a spiritual plane. Didactic suffering is a major legacy from the story of Christ and in Christian tragedy is not confined to one climactic episode. The hero suffers from beginning to end.

More significant for American Christian tragedy is the new kind of anagnorisis it portrays, the spiritual recognition of self. This is done in two concomitant ways. First, the tragic hero must discover, not that he is a sinner or culprit, but that he is finite and vulnerable; that he is a small representative of the race and must fulfill his human responsibilities.

Secondly, the catastrophes of most of our tragic heroes are punishments. No matter how much an American tragic writer would love to place the blame on blind fate, or what goes for blind fate today—heredity, society, sex—he cannot conform to the Greek manner. Obeisance to Christian teaching demands at least an ostensible tandem of crime and punishment, and this the American tragedian gives us. It is something more concrete than pride, the catchall sin of Christianity. Arthur Dimmesdale is an adulterer and a fraud; Billy Budd kills a man; Santiago goes too far and kills one of nature's creatures. Yet, never are we allowed to feel either the rectitude or certitude of this sequence of events. The crimes are only technically sins; we allow for man's original condition. In the sphere of choice only, not in the actual act, lie the sources of guilt. Thus, in its reach for catharsis, American tragedy utilizes the Christian paradox of guilt divorced from sin. Pity for the hero and terror about our condition are aroused because the protagonist is condemned for his natural fallibility. In such a situation, we pity the hero and feel terror for ourselves when we witness a good man suffer and perhaps even die for natural fallibility.

WE SINNED ALL

Attempting to demonstrate how close Hawthorne's *Scarlet Letter* (1850) was to Aristotelian tragic form, as adapted by Shakespeare, Malcolm Cowley has suggested:

> [Hawthorne] has presented us with distinguished, even noble, characters who are inevitably brought to grief for having violated the laws of heaven and the tribe. He has presented "an action that is serious and also, as having magnitude, complete in itself . . . with incidents arousing pity and fear, wherewith to accomplish its catharsis of such emotions." . . . It is not too much to say that he had recaptured, for his New England, the essence of Greek tragedy.[22]

In pure structure, Cowley ingeniously goes on to show, Hawthorne emulated the tragic form of the Elizabethan successors to the Greeks by casting his tragedy into five acts.

But truly, neither the dramatis personae nor the plot has magnitude in either the Aristotelian or Shakespearean sense. We have no princes, powers, or potentates here. The town of Boston hardly shudders because of this domestic tragedy, as Venice does in *Othello*. Wherein lies the magnitude of this little, self-contained, unassuming sordid tale

---

22. Malcolm Cowley, "Five Acts of *The Scarlet Letter*," in Nathaniel Hawthorne, *The Scarlet Letter*, ed. Sculley Bradley *et al.* (Critical ed.; New York: W. W. Norton, 1962), 330.

of adultery? The answer lies in understanding that the heaven Cowley alludes to, whose laws were violated in *The Scarlet Letter*, does not rest on Mount Olympus, but on Sinai and Calvary. Though glimpses of classical tragedy are perceptible in the novel and must be considered in any discussion of its import as a tragedy, Hawthorne's world is not the pagan world, and his tragic tradition is not the myths of Prometheus or Oedipus or the house of Atreus, as in later American tragedy. The primal tragic myth for Hawthorne is the catastrophe of Adam.[23]

In August of the year *The Scarlet Letter* was published, the coalescence of these two traditions was recognized in some of Hawthorne's short stories by Herman Melville, who himself was then struggling to control the confluence of these two legacies. In his review of *Mosses from an Old Manse*, Melville equated Hawthorne with Shakespeare, tracing their tragic vision to "that Calvinistic sense of Innate Depravity and Original Sin from whose visitation in some shape or other no thinking man is always and wholly free." Shakespeare, Melville says, expressed this dark understanding "through the mouths of the dark characters of Hamlet, Timon, Lear, and Iago." [24] What a mixed bag of characters this is—grand and little heroes and villains! Yet it is particularly astute in connection with Hawthorne, who had the combination of Calvinism and humanism, the horror of sin and pity for the sinners, and the terror of Puritan determinism and love of a moral God to see the destined Hamlet and Lear, the hateful maledictory Timon, and the

23. For parallel assertions see Lewis, *The American Adam*, Chap. 6, which deals, however, but little with *The Scarlet Letter*; and Roy R. Male, *Hawthorne's Tragic Vision* (1957; reprint, New York: W. W. Norton, 1964), 8, 14, *passim*, but Male's chapter on the novel (6) emphasizes elements of tragedy other than those in this book.

24. Herman Melville, "Hawthorne and His Mosses," in Willard Thorp (ed.), *Herman Melville: Representative Selections* (New York: American Book Co., 1938), 333, 334.

vile, villainous, and monstrous Iago *all* sharing in the mimesis of tragic destiny.

The Calvinistic sense of depravity and necessity originates, of course, in the story of Adam and Eve, sin symbolized there as in *The Scarlet Letter* by natural sexuality. Certainly, Hawthorne could not escape the Puritan teaching that "In Adam's fall / We sinned all," but that aphorism leads to a doctrine of such fatalism that it is beyond the pale of tragedy. The dogma needed the corrective of humanism, and that was provided by John Milton's treatment of the story. Perhaps the most important aspect of this myth of humanity that Milton offered his American beneficiary was the purposefulness of the primal sin. When Milton allows Adam to follow his nature rather than his intellect, the heart rather than the head, the natural, original sin is consecrated. But it is not the consecration of the sin as an act—this is the mistake that Hester Prynne makes. It is the vision of moral purpose in the consequences of the sin that consecrates it. Hawthorne is talking of the sphere of choice, not the act of choice. In *Paradise Lost*, this perception is validated in the vision vouchsafed to Adam at the end of the poem. It will come to Hawthorne's Adam, Arthur Dimmesdale, in his final speech at the end of the novel.

The fall of Adam is, of course, not the only enactment of a tragedy of "triumphant ignominy" that the Christian tradition offered Hawthorne. There is Christ himself who was afflicted because of a foreordained divine plan. First and last, it is this doubleness of the Christological story that Hawthorne had in mind and that refracted his tragic vision when he wrote *The Scarlet Letter*. At the beginning of the novel, Hawthorne uses the Christ story to explode his plot onto a stage infinitely higher and broader than the confines of old Boston. We discover Hester and Pearl on the scaffold before an almost entirely hostile audience, most of whom are muttering complaints against the magistrates for washing their hands of Hester so readily. The echo of Pilate and the populace is not too farfetched, for it follows upon the surprising comparison that Hawthorne makes between this tableau and "the image of Divine Maternity, which so many illustrious painters have vied with one another to represent" (Chapter 2, p. 56).[25] And if any reader is ready to restrict this image merely to an oversentimental connection, Hawthorne does not permit it: the scene is "something which should remind [one], indeed, but only by contrast, of the sacred image of sinless motherhood, whose infant was to redeem the world" (Chapter 2, p. 56). Hawthorne sounds here like the shrewd lawyer who makes his point upon the jury with an illegal ploy in the courtroom. The effect, though illegal, is not lost. He has successfully— if by contrast only—implanted in his reader's mind the whole Christological nexus of divine determinism and catastrophe, of redemption through tragedy.

A religious concept of tragedy is conjoined in Hawthorne's mind with a philosophical concept of determinism. Hawthorne has Arthur Dimmesdale perceive God's handiwork in sending punishment for his sin. He thus characterizes Chillingworth as an instrument of God, as well as of the devil, and in the conclusion places the whole action at the throne of the Deity.

Philosophically, Peter Thorslev tells us, Hawthorne modified the absolute Calvinistic determinism. The pure determinist postulates "for every event in the physical or psychical world . . . a necessary and sufficient cause." But this cause is not supernatural: "A consistent determinist

---

25. Nathaniel Hawthorne, *The Scarlet Letter*, ed. William Charvat *et al.* (Centenary ed.; Columbus: Ohio State University Press, 1962). References to the text of the novel will be in parentheses and include both page of the Centenary edition and chapter for the convenience of readers with other editions.

would deny divine interposition in the causal chain of
events." The pure fatalist, on the other hand, sees life as an
a-causal existence, thwarting and interrupting an orderly
sequence of events "by the interposition of a purposeful
agency called God, Fate, or Destiny." [26] Somewhere in between is Hawthorne. From the fatalist he takes the notion
of a purposeful agency called God, but denies the notions
of a-causality and disarray in the affairs of men. From the
determinist he accepts the notion of a necessary and sufficient cause, but rejects the denial of divine interposition and
the amorality that is seen in the affairs of men.

Consequently, Thorslev summarizes, Hawthorne "portrays the maximum of guilt with the minimum of responsibility." From this philosophical stance, Hawthorne creates stories in which we see "his de-emphasis of the moment
of decision and his diminution of the relative freedom of
the will . . . [which] lend his novels their pervasive gloom,
their air of 'dark necessity,' and their tragic pathos." [27] In
the story of the aftermath of adultery, Hawthorne found an
adequate vehicle for the communication of this tragic concept. Adultery, though an act of passion and perhaps of
love, is an act of volition, a forgetfulness of God's law and
man's, and must, like Adam's destined sin, be punished. Arthur never denies the sinfulness of his momentary weakness of character, frailty of judgment, or whatever tragic
flaw best applies. But Hawthorne's concept of determinism
awakens the question that perhaps there was one step prior
to that first step awry. Perhaps it was a decision in heaven
that originated the enactment and that gives rectitude to
the ascension of all these characters—Arthur and Hester
and Chillingworth, too—when all is concluded.

26. Peter Thorslev, "Hawthorne's Determinism: An Analysis," *Nineteenth-Century Fiction*, XIX (September, 1964), 144, 145, 148.
27. *Ibid.*, 150, 156.

The structure and the vision into which they are cast are the amalgamated legacies of classical and biblical literature. For the tragic hero we shall turn back to Aristotle. For the tragic plot, we shall turn to the story of Jesus and the Book of Job.

It must be admitted that Hawthorne, in fulfilling Aristotelian prerequisites of peripety and anagnorisis, receives little ostensible help from his chief characters, none of whom is a traditional tragic hero. Of the four major figures in *The Scarlet Letter*—Hester Prynne, Arthur Dimmesdale, Roger Chillingworth, and little Pearl—the first is a sentimental romantic, the second a weakling, the third a diabolical villain, and the last an impish child. It is not a rich cast for the accolade of tragic heroism. Actually, however, it is part of Hawthorne's American type of tragic vision that his characters gain nobility not by reason of status, but in proportion to the growing recognition by themselves and the reader that they are involved in an enactment of magnitude, that they have a responsibility beyond the narrowness of self, that they have importance in the scheme of things that transcends the immediate situation, and that they are predetermined, yet free enough to fulfill their responsibility.

Despite Richard Sewall's valiant exposition of her as a tragic heroine, for several reasons catharsis cannot result from Hester Prynne. First, her career goes the opposite way and thus evokes the wrong response. We cannot respond to the type of suffering that Hawthorne demonstrates for us. Hester falls from no height; when we meet her, she is already fallen. In Chapter 2 she is already at the nadir of her young, vibrant life. Far from the peripety that Aristotle rightly saw as a condition of tragic plot, the story of Hester from the first is upward. Even the scarlet letter "A" becomes the symbol for "Able" and "Angel," and by the end of the story she has become a living, respected legend. Certainly she suffered. But suffering per se is only spectacle (*Poetics*, Chapter 11) and not enough in itself to evoke pity and terror. Indeed, we admire, more than pity her, for her stoicism. Moreover, the fact is that she is not a protagonist of the action. Henry James observed that Hester soon recedes into being merely "an accessory figure." [28] She is external to the core of the plot. Once Chillingworth appears on the scene, she is outside the intrigue between the minister and the physician.

The corollary of the primal sin in which Hester and Arthur are involved questions the matter of guilt in the commission of sin, as far as Hawthorne is concerned. We see that in his touch of irony that goes beyond Milton. In Genesis and *Paradise Lost*, it is the serpent who causes the Fall; in *The Scarlet Letter*, the serpentine character Chillingworth serves as the righteous, if hateful, avenging Fury—and undergoes suffering for it! In this role, the satanic figure serves the meaning and pattern of Hawthorne's tragedy. For all his loathsomeness, Roger Chillingworth offers stronger credentials as a tragic figure. First, he suffers a peripety of sorts, from stalwart, respected scientist to deformed monomaniac. Secondly, this monomania, a flaw of character, is the cause of his descent. He is, in fact, an Iago type, but with a number of mitigating circumstances. Though he is a villain—indeed, he commits the unpardonable sin (yet Hawthorne, before he writes the last page of *The Scarlet Letter* will forgive him!); though he is a treacherous friend and violates the sanctity of natural love, yet he is not the prime cause of his evil. He himself is dehumanized to perform a necessary act of revenge, and like most tragic figures, he suffers and understands. In two signifi-

28. Henry James, *Hawthorne* (1879; reprint, Ithaca, N.Y.: Cornell University Press, 1966), 89.

cant speeches to Hester, he reveals the extent of his perception. He sees himself as part of the divine plan. Early in the novel, in their prison interview, he says to her: "Think not that I shall interfere with Heaven's own method of retribution, or, to my own loss, betray him to the gripe of human law" (Chapter 4, p. 75).

Later, years later, in the forest when Hester tries to persuade him from his vengeful probing, Chillingworth reminds Hester that she has the wrong slant and that he is destined to his role in the tragedy: " 'Peace, Hester, peace!' replied the old man, with gloomy sternness. 'It is not granted me to pardon. I have no such power as thou tellest me of. . . . Neither am I fiend-like, who have snatched a fiend's office from his hands. It is our fate. Let the black flower blossom as it may!' " (Chapter 14, p. 174).

Hawthorne himself testifies that Chillingworth's grasp of the cosmic implications of his role in the affair of Arthur and Hester is correct. He tells us that "Providence—using the avenger and the victim for its own purposes, and, perchance, pardoning where it seemed most to punish—had substituted for [Chillingworth's] black devices" (Chapter 11, pp. 139–40). Fated by divine plan to this nefarious task, Chillingworth is given "divine permission, for a season, to burrow into the clergyman's intimacy, and plot against his soul" (Chapter 9, p. 128). A theological villain, Chillingworth is an earthly victim!

His opposite, Arthur Dimmesdale, is also a poor candidate for tragic heroism. For much of the story, he is rather a weakling, and we wonder who seduced whom on that fateful night a year before the story opens. As in the myth in Genesis, Arthur-Adam hides himself, and thus Hawthorne preserves the element of free will in his tragedy. Arthur's sin and subsequent conduct and Chillingworth's "black devices" are free acts. But both characters have the nature to be selected for their respective roles in a pattern of necessity toward a determined tragic end. That is the paradoxical but essential point of the enactment that Hawthorne emphasizes after we have witnessed the peripety of the minister and his years of suffering. Finally Arthur-Christ undergoes the ultimate torture and epiphany—anagnorisis—at the moment before he dies.

The organic interaction of the chief personae may be better understood by reference to the biblical tragedy that had a rather deep effect on Hawthorne, the Book of Job.[29] But we must be careful to limit what relationship there is between this tragedy and *The Scarlet Letter*. It is not in theme, it seems to me. *The Scarlet Letter* is not a story of unjust divine affliction: all three adults in the tale are sinners, and all admit it to some extent. It seems to me that Hawthorne was awed by the operation of divine selection of a hero, so close to the predeterminism of Calvinism, and by the paradoxical pattern of the plot which reveals that those friends who tried to divert Job from the fulfillment of God's design are not friends at all, but tempters and antagonists.

"Heaven hath granted thee," Arthur cries to Hester early in the novel, "an open ignominy, that thereby thou mayest work out an open triumph over the evil within thee, and the sorrow without. Take heed how thou deniest to him who, perchance, hath not the courage to grasp it for himself —the bitter, but wholesome, cup that is now presented to thy lips!" (Chapter 3, p. 67).

Secrecy is but the first in a series of temptations that Ar-

29. Austin Warren, "Hawthorne's Reading," *New England Quarterly*, VIII (December, 1935), 493–94, reports James T. Fields's comment: "It was a great pleasure to hear [Hawthorne] talk about the Book of Job"; Luther Mansfield and H. P. Vincent, editors of the Centenary edition of *Moby-Dick* (New York: Hendricks House, 1952), in their "Explanatory Notes," 699–700, hear a distinct echo from the Book of Job in *The Scarlet Letter*.

thur is required to undergo, submission to any one of which could have ended the enactment abruptly. We must understand that these temptations are part of the dark necessity of the tragic enactment, or we shall wonder forevermore why Arthur lacks courage for seven years and then suddenly finds it. Perhaps we can see an evolution in these temptations.

The second one involves Pearl. At the midnight reunion on the scaffold, Arthur holds his daughter's hand, and when she tries to pull it away, he holds it fast "a moment longer" out of love. Then:

> "But wilt thou promise," asked Pearl, "to take my hand and mother's hand, tomorrow noontide?"
> "Not then, Pearl," said the minister, "but another time!"
> "And what other time?" persisted the child.
> "At the great judgment day!" whispered the minister. ". . . But the daylight of this world shall not see our meeting." (Chapter 12, p. 153)

After the sign in the sky, Pearl "withdrew her hand," and the moment of temptation to gain his daughter's love ends.

The third temptation is Chillingworth's, who offers Dimmesdale surcease from self-torture. For awhile it appeared as if poor Dimmesdale hoped that Chillingworth's concoctions would help him, as if his purgatory were susceptible to earthly ministrations. Arthur learns finally that Chillingworth was intent all along on his own brand of vengeance, whatever else Heaven might do. When Arthur throws himself on God's mercy, for which end God used Chillingworth's evil machinations, it is then that the old man murmurs, "Thou hast escaped me! . . . Thou hast escaped me!" (Chapter 23, p. 256). So this temptation, too, is suffered and overcome.

The ultimate temptation occurs in the forest when Hester Prynne lets down her hair and after eight years thrills with the vibrancy of Eve. Though certainly she does not counsel blasphemy, like Job's wife, she does counsel escape. And for a time the temptation of freedom with Hester intoxicates the poor minister. On the way home, he almost yields to little impious temptations to whisper deviltries into innocent ears. Presently he catches himself. " 'What is it that haunts and tempts me thus?' cried the minister to himself. . . . 'Am I mad? or am I given over utterly to the fiend? Did I make a contract with him in the forest, and sign it with my blood?' " (Chapter 20, p. 220).

This is rather a striking, if unwitting, insight into the forest encounter with Hester. He had been "tempted by a dream of happiness, [and] he had yielded himself with deliberate choice, as he had never done before to what he knew was deadly sin" (Chapter 20, p. 222). The mood passes, and Arthur comes to realize that even this final and most dangerous temptation was necessary for his moral evolution. He is now able, after so much suffering, "to stand apart, and eye [his] former self with scornful, pitying, but half-envious curiosity. That self was gone! Another man had returned from the forest; a wiser one; with a knowledge of hidden mysteries which the simplicity of the former never could have reached. A bitter kind of knowledge that!" (Chapter 20, p. 223). Arthur Dimmesdale stands on the verge of that moment of mysterious knowing what life is all about.

At this point, after experiencing the fall of Adam and suffering of Job, Arthur dies like Christ. In the final utterance that he composed for the Reverend Arthur Dimmesdale in *The Scarlet Letter*, Nathaniel Hawthorne culminates the development of his concept of tragedy. Cries Dimmesdale to the attendant crowd: "God knows; and He is merciful! He hath proved his mercy, most of all, in my afflictions. By giving me this burning torture to bear upon my breast! By sending yonder dark and terrible old man, to keep the torture always at red heat! By bringing me hither to die this death of triumphant ignominy before the people! Had either of these agonies been wanting, I had been lost forever! Praised be his name! His will be done! Farewell!" (Chapter 23, pp. 256–57).

Dimmesdale's dying gestures and words "are so recorded as to remind us of Christ on the cross," observes Hyatt Waggoner.[30] The *agon* here, however, goes beyond mere suggestion. The tableau is very much like the crucifixion scene of the Gospels: the stricken central figure in a posture of ignominy, surrounded by a restless, awed crowd, and attended by a small band of loved ones. Yet the horrid, shameful death is triumphant because it is didactic, ennobling, and destined. Not even Christ was free. He had his cross to bear. The glory of God is proclaimed in both enactments.

Hawthorne, like earlier Judeo-Christian tragedians who were his masters, cannot let it alone. Morality must parallel determinism. Ascension must be acknowledged. Job is rewarded in the epilogue to that book. Christ is resurrected. Hamlet's soul flies upward on the song of angels, as Horatio says. Milton permits Adam to envision ultimate redemption. Here Dimmesdale and Chillingworth, together with Hester, join them (Chapter 24, p. 260). It is not theology that matters here, but catharsis. Hawthorne wrote out of a consciousness that saw a world in which humans who discover love may be rewarded with suffering; in which the beloved is a spiritual antagonist and the hated one a spiritual partner; in which suffering is a didactic instrument; in which the catharsis turns topsy-turvy our naïve, terrestrial conceptions of good and evil, innocence and guilt. It is right

---

30. Hyatt Waggoner, "Art and Belief," in Roy Harvey Pearce (ed.), *Hawthorne: Centenary Essays* (Columbus: Ohio State University Press, 1964), 191.

for Hawthorne, with such a concept of tragic vision and form, to ask for pity for these people and to leave us the terror of perceiving what chained them to one another.

YOUNG JESUS

Forty years later, in 1891, Herman Melville fixed on the face of Billy Budd the mask of Christ in the American tragedy that more than any other acutely and incisively depicts the paradox of Christian tragedy. The tale is a theological allegory. The king of England is not merely terrestrial royalty, but the absent, distant, omnipotent Deity; Billy is not only a handsome foretopman, but an innocent, flawed Adam and a condemned Jesus; Captain Vere is a Pilate who cannot wash his hands of him; and Claggert is not only a malicious villain beset by a tumultuous subconscious, but a sundered demon pendulating between Christ and Satan.

The providence and power of the surrogate deity become evident as Melville develops the background of the story. It is not enough to set the tale on shipboard, where the captain is normally an absolute chieftain. It is not even enough to impose upon this the situation that the ship is involved in a war, which strengthens the absoluteness of the distant, absent monarch's shipboard law and the smallness of the individual's right of life and existence. Upon all this Melville superimposes a mutiny, which effectively squashes all rights and narrows the passages of decision—not only by an august captain but also by lowly crew members. When one is born into the fallible condition of humanity, Melville ironically implies, he loses the Rights of Man (the name of the ship *from* which Billy is impressed) and takes on the onerous responsibilities of man to complete the meaning of his sovereign as Indomitable (the name of the ship that Billy is impressed *into*). By such twists of Christian irony is Melville's tragic vision refracted.

Billy, the near-perfect specimen of mankind, earns the love of captain, officers, and crew, save one—the master-at-arms whose enmity he does not earn, but attracts. This petty officer falsely accuses Billy of mutinous intentions and in a face-to-face confrontation is struck dead by the angelic Handsome Sailor. The drumhead court convened to judge the matter is inclined to compromise on the sentence of the homicide, but is persuaded by the captain's argument, based on the incendiariness of the situation, to hand down a death sentence. In the dawn's early light, Billy Budd is hanged.

That this *agon* is not a mere figment of historical romance, Melville attests by the characterizations and interrelationships of the three members of the crew directly concerned—Billy Budd, Captain Vere, and John Claggart. In Melville's tragic vision, natural goodness still exists, is believable, and is tragic, but natural depravity is equally tragic. He characterizes Billy "an angel of God," endowed with "welkin eyes" and innocence. "Who was your father?" an officer asks him. "God knows, Sir," Billy ingenuously replies (298).[31] The mystery of birth applies not only to Jesus but to Adam, of course, and Melville writes of Billy: "By his original constitution aided by the cooperating influence of his lot, Billy in many respects, was little more than a sort of upright barbarian, much such as Adam presumably might have been ere the urbane serpent wriggled himself into his company" (299).

But he is not perfect. He stammers—the one flaw which conjoins him to humanity: "The avowal of such an imperfection in the Handsome Sailor should be evidence not

31. *Billy Budd, Foretopman*, in Richard Chase (ed.), *Herman Melville: Selected Tales and Poems* (New York: Rinehart, 1959). Page numbers of this edition are cited in the text in parentheses.

alone that he is not presented as a conventional hero, but also that the story in which he is the main figure is not romance" (300). No, Billy is a hero neither of a conventional novel nor of a romance. All that is left to him is the painful heroism of a tragedy. He is, as his captain calls him, a "fated boy" (344).

After the serpent, Claggart, does his nefarious wriggling, Billy stands before his captain accused, and the latter's fatherly concern brings to Billy's "face an expression which was a crucifixion to behold" (344). A generation earlier Melville masked Captain Ahab's face also with a crucifixion. I shall discuss the implications of that allusion in the following chapter. In Captain Vere's argument for the necessity of a capital sentence, Melville recapitulates the allegorical hints strewn throughout the story that Billy's tragedy is the tragedy of humanity in an encounter with the power of the Creator. Is "our allegiance . . . to Nature?" he asks the court trying Billy. "No, to the King. . . . In receiving due commissions we in the most important regards ceased to be natural free agents" (356). Billy, alias Adam, alias Jesus, is condemned, of course. As he is hanged before the ship's company, heaven sends forth a sign: "At the same moment it chanced that the vapory fleece hanging low in the East, was shot through with the soft glory as of the fleece of the Lamb of God seen in nuptial union and simultaneously therewith, watched by the wedged mass of upturned faces, Billy ascended; and ascending, took the full rose of the dawn" (367).

The communal sacrifice is done; the didactic catastrophe of a hero whose "noble descent was as evident in him as in a blood horse" (298) has been witnessed here as it had been at that earlier Crucifixion nearly 1900 years before, and at every tragic catastrophe since. The mast on which Billy had been hanged becomes the sailors' relic: "To them a chip of it was as a piece of the cross" (374).

What urged the rude sailors to this paroxysm of instinctive worship? What urged the untutored Billy Budd to vindicate his captain's insistence upon his death by shouting as his last words, "God Bless Captain Vere!"? What anagnorisis did they arrive at? It is the sense of tragic mystery in God's world. "Ay, there is a mystery," says Captain Vere to the court, "but to use a Scriptural phrase, it is 'a mystery of iniquity', a matter for psychological theologians to discuss" (352).

It is significant that Melville seems to spend more time on the mystery of Claggart's iniquity, his unmotivated hatred of the Handsome Sailor, than on the mystery of Billy's innocence. Iniquity is perhaps the more fascinating pursuit of understanding, because it is stark reality. Melville comments: "The cause, necessarily to be assumed as the sole one assignable, is in its very realism as much changed with the prime element of Radcliffian romance, the *mysteriousness*. . . . For what can more partake of the mysteriousness than an antipathy spontaneous and profound such as is evoked in certain exceptional mortals by the mere aspect of some other mortal, however harmless he may be? If not called forth by this harmlessness itself?" (319).

There is nothing more mysterious than evil, and Melville, awed and bewildered by the thrust of his vision, like William Blake contemplating the tiger, must place the whole mystery at its place of origin: "One person excepted [Captain Vere], the master-at-arms was perhaps the only man in the ship intellectually capable of adequately appreciating the moral phenomenon presented in Billy Budd . . . [but he must] like the scorpion for which the Creator alone is responsible, act out to the end the part allotted to it"

(324). Claggart's iniquity is a " 'Natural Depravity: a depravity according to nature.' A definition which though savoring of Calvinism, by no means involves Calvin's dogma as to total mankind. Evidently its intent makes it applicable but to individuals" (321).

The suffering experienced in the story is more the villain's than the hero's, which is not really surprising. Billy is at first too innocent to know what he is about to lose. But Claggart suffers from his first glimpse of innocence. Regardless of his depravity, he responds, and he suffers the Sturm und Drang in his spirit: "Then would Claggart look like the man of sorrows. Yes, and sometimes the melancholy expression would have in it a touch of soft yearning, as if Claggart could even have loved Billy but for fate and ban. But this was an evanescence, and quickly repented of, as it were, by an immitigable look, pinching and shrivelling the visage with the momentary semblance of a wrinkled walnut" (333). The original mask on Claggart's face, however, was the mask of Christ, "the man of sorrows."

Thus God creates men's natures that He needs to complete His inscrutable purposes. The tragedy, Melville tells us, is dependent upon the natural innocence of one Billy Budd and the natural depravity of one John Claggart—and any deviation from their natures would have voided the enactment. Both are placed in a fated covenant with God and, Melville bitterly adds, with each other. Thus the act of tragedy is the act of necessity. Speculate how we will, it is "the prisoner's deed—with that we have to do," says Captain Vere (352). Billy, we must not forget, killed a man. Even so, we are not assuaged when Vere intones: "Before a court less arbitrary and more merciful than a martial one that plea would largely extenuate. At the last Assizes it shall acquit. But how here? We proceed under the law of the Mutiny Act. In feature no child can resemble his father more than that Act resembles in spirit the thing from which it derives—War" (356). The power of the catharsis is not allayed. Ascension, divine redemption, heavenly reward notwithstanding, Christian tragedy does not look beyond the catastrophe for the effect. The tragedy of our existence is the stuff of its drama.

But if one were to think that *Billy Budd* is an exercise in existential despair, Melville hastens to set the record straight. This is Christian tragedy he is writing. Whatever passed between Billy and Captain Vere when he delivered the sentence of death is unreported, but we may infer that it was enough to deepen Billy's insight into this our life. His anagnorisis is so deep, in fact, that he does not need the theological succor of the chaplain, but comes to religious serenity with the realization of his own condition, and Captain Vere's, and perhaps even Claggart's, and cries out as the noose is pulled, "God Bless Captain Vere!"

If this is not enough, Melville appends the incident in which the *Indomitable* sinks the *Atheiste* and Vere dies with Billy's name on his lips. God not only lives, but prevails.

OLD CHRIST

In *Green Hills of Africa* (1935), though he did not know it, the configuration of a tragic novella formed in Ernest Hemingway's imagination: "When, on the sea, you are along with it and know that this Gulf Stream you are living with, knowing, learning about, and loving, has moved, as it moves, since before man . . . the things you find out about it, and those that have always lived in it, are permanent and of value because that stream will flow as it had flowed." [32] The glimmerings of a terror that one day will

32. Quoted by Carlos Baker, *Hemingway: The Writer as Artist* (Princeton, N.J.: Princeton University Press, 1956), 324.

quietly infuse the catharsis of *The Old Man and the Sea*
seventeen years later are perceptible here in the unceasing
flow of time and power in the sea. Hemingway raises no
question of man's victory over this power, for the eternality
of its constant flow symbolizes unassailability. The problem
is living, learning, and loving—a Christian sequence of life.

As with a number of American tragic heroes, we discover
Santiago at the very nadir of his peripety. Of all the fisher-
men on his beach, only the old man suffers the indignity of
eighty-four days without a fish. It would seem that he, only
he, was being primed for the lonely enactment out there
on the sea, arbitrarily chosen, because of his past success,
righteous pride, and humble virtue, to suffer the attention
of omnipotent natural forces. There is nothing small about
this tragic enactment, except the man. The sea is immense,
and the marlin he catches, the largest and noblest of mar-
lins. In stark ritualistic detail, Hemingway describes how
Santiago priestlike prepared for the day's fishing, how he
lowered the lines, how he hooked the marlin, how he played
with the hooked fish to secure him, how the sharks attacked
and stripped the carcass because that is their function in
the sea, how Santiago tried to save the fish and could not.
An aura of holiness hangs over this succession of enacted
rites. Santiago's isolation on the sea is so complete that the
coast guard search planes miss him and his skiff. At the end,
after he lands the skeleton, nobody from the town, not even
the boy Manolin, is around to witness or to aid Santiago up
the hill to his hut.

Hemingway must be admired for the realistic way in
which he infuses commonplace anecdote with tragic possibility, with no leap or jarring of the reader's sensibility.
"The old Greeks," remarked J. Donald Adams, ". . . would
have liked and understood Hemingway's handling of his
story. . . . Hemingway has, in this tale, got back to litera-

ture's roots in epic and folksong." [33] The old Greeks would have liked *Old Man* because they would have recognized in Santiago a tyrannos after their own hearts—lowborn and inarticulate, but afflicted with the tragic mixture of arbitrary selection, fate, choice, and anagnorisis.

But Greek heroism is not the major archetype for *The Old Man and the Sea*. It seems here to be the last vestigial gasp of the romantic heroism that characterized Hemingway's earlier and younger heroes like Frederic Henry and Robert Jordan. Now the hero is an old Christ who "reflects Job-like," said Carlos Baker, "on the problem of the connection between sin and sufficiency"—an old man "too human not to be troubled, like Job, before him." [34]

> . . . Do not think about sin, he thought. There are enough problems now without sin. Also I have no understanding of it.
> I have no understanding of it and I am not sure that I believe in it. Perhaps it was sin to kill the fish. I suppose it was even though I did it to keep me alive and feed many people. But then everything is a sin. Do not think about sin. It is much too late for that and there are people who are paid to do it. . . . You did not kill the fish only to keep alive and sell for food, he thought. You killed him for pride and because you are a fisherman. You loved him when he was alive and you loved him after. If you love him, it is not a sin to kill him. Or is it more? (115–16)[35]

This is Hemingway's agreement with American tragedy's gloss on Christian doctrine: sin can be without guilt, and guilt can be divorced from sin. Santiago is right in trying not to think about it, for it is a conundrum suited to other heroes in other climes, not to commonplace twentieth-

33. J. Donald Adams, "Speaking of Books," *New York Times Book Review*, September 21, 1952, Sec. 7, p. 2.
34. Baker, *Writer as Artist*, 307, 316.
35. Ernest Hemingway, *The Old Man and the Sea* (New York: Scribner's, 1952). Page references will be given in the text in parentheses.

century heroes, to reconcile. That sin still exists and exacts
its toll and that guilt, not engendered by freely committed
sin, exists and exacts its toll are enough of an anagnorisis
of the human situation.

Arbitrarily selected, Santiago chooses to enter what, unbeknownst to him, is a covenant of tragedy. "His [the great
fish's] choice had been to stay in the deep dark water far
out beyond the snares and traps and treacheries. My choice
was to go there to find him beyond all the people. Beyond
all the people in the world. Now we are joined together and
have been since noon. And no one to help either of us" (55).
Clinton Burhans' comment on this point, "The old man
learns the sin into which men inevitably fall by going far
out beyond their depth, their true place in life," [36] is incomprehensible. The whole point of Hemingway's tragedy
is that the true place in the life of a tragic hero is inevitably
out there beyond his depth—that is what he was born for.
Can such a fated act, committed ironically by Santiago's
choice because destiny knew this would be his choice—can
such a fated act be a sin? Every Christ in the Bible taught
otherwise.

Santiago is caught up in the classic problem of the sphere
of choice versus the act of choice, and Hemingway's Christian tragedy ordains him into a sphere of tragic action only.
It is rather difficult to see in the nature of Santiago, at the
juncture in life when we catch him, succumbing to the flaw
of hubris, as Malcolm Cowley claims.[37] Rather, he is steadfast in humility before the natural forces that face him:
"He was too simple to wonder when he had attained humility. But he knew he had attained it and he knew it was

36. Clinton S. Burhans, Jr., "*Old Man and the Sea*: Hemingway's Tragic
Vision of Man," *American Literature*, XXX (1960), 447.
37. Malcolm Cowley, "Hemingway's Novel Has the Rich Simplicity of a
Classic," *New York Herald-Tribune Book Review*, September 7, 1952, p. 1.

not disgraceful and it carried no loss of true pride" (14). No hero afflicted with hubris speaks this way. This is Christian humility, bereft of the simplistic Christian certainty of defining sin and guilt.

Hemingway's vision of Santiago sees him as a ritualistic and didactic figure of crucified guiltlessness. After the ritual of fishing, after the battle of the tragic *isolato* against the natural forces that limit his individualism, after the rapacious agents of those forces, the sharks, strip the marlin of all the meat between the head and the tail (the alpha and the omega?), Santiago wearily leans back in his skiff, the palms of his hands bloodied by the fishing line, his forehead raw from the sun, stunned but not defeated. There is one more ritual to perform.

He brings his skiff to harbor and detaches the mast from the boat. Gethsemane having been reenacted on the sea, the Crucifixion awaits. "He shouldered the mast and started to climb" the hill to his hut. "At the top he fell and lay some time with the mast across his shoulder." He tries to get up, but cannot. Then he lays the mast down, gets up, lifts the mast, and "put[s] it on his shoulder and start[s] up the road," his via dolorosa to Calvary. In the hut, he collapses on his cot and sleeps with "his arms straight out and the palms up" (133–34). His passion ends in a "climax of silence," through which, Karl Jaspers said, "tragedy suggests and brings to realization the highest possibilities of man." [38]

The mime and the posture, it has often been noted, are indeed Christological. Philip Young recalls what the Crucifixion meant to Hemingway in a playlet the latter had written back in 1926, *Today Is Friday*. The refrain uttered over and over again by the amazed Roman soldier in the guard-

38. Karl Jaspers, "Tragedy Is Not Enough," in Michel and Sewall (eds.), *Modern Essays*, 6.

room after the event is: "He was pretty good in there today."[39]

Santiago suffers a didactic catastrophe, not too dissimilar to Christ's. The meaning of his catastrophe flows into the boy Manolin, the old man's disciple. Manolin is Santiago's companion before the tragic enactment, and he is there to serve the hero after he is crucified. He is constantly in Santiago's mind, even during the battle with the marlin and the sharks. Especially at the nadir of his bleak consideration of the human condition: "Besides, [Santiago] thought, everything kills everything else in some way. Fishing kills exactly as it keeps me alive. The boy keeps me alive, he thought. I must not deceive myself too much" (117). Of course, it will be the boy who will keep Santiago figuratively alive after he has truly died,[40] for Manolin learns Santiago's lessons well. Early in the story, he had learned the need for faith (11) and the fact that there are things a man must do. After the *agon* on the sea, Santiago says, "They beat me, Manolin. . . . They truly beat me," and the boy replies significantly, "*He* didn't beat you. Not the fish" (136). No, Santiago's defeat is not wasted; Manolin has learned who "they" are, and it is not the poor marlin. With the dauntless spirit he emulates from his master, the boy refuses to dwell on the theme of defeat. After all, they have not been killed altogether. He says to Santiago:

> "Now we must make our plans about other things."
> "No. I am not lucky. I am not lucky anymore."
> "The hell with luck," the boy said. "I'll bring the luck with me." (137)

39. Philip Young, *Ernest Hemingway* (New York: Rinehart, 1952), 101.
40. Beckford Sylvester, "They Went Through This Fiction Every Day: Informed Illusion in *Old Man and the Sea*," *Modern Fiction Studies*, XII (1966), 467, argues for the death of Santiago at the end of the novella. Young, *Hemingway*, 95, among the majority, predicts he will "fish again another day."

With this simple piece of dialogue, Hemingway pushes the catharsis beyond our pity for Santiago and terror of the secret cause that agonized him. For we remember Santiago's comment on his luck just a few pages before: "You violated your luck," he said to himself, "when you went out too far" (128). And here we see young Manolin starting out on that glorious but painful voyage of life that will lead him to tragedy. Like Hemingway's description of the Gulf Stream that seeded the growth of *The Old Man and the Sea*, "that stream will flow as it had flowed." Each generation must have its hero who will don the mask of Christ and go up to be crucified. This is the ultimate catharsis of Christian tragedy.

III

The Mask of Satan

Indeed, the implications of Christian teaching contributed to American tragedy not only sympathetic heroes, but also hateful protagonists, diabolical villains with Christological veneers who turn out to be heroes. Dimmesdale's antagonist, "Satan's emissary," Roger Chillingworth, and Billy's, the "naturally depraved" diabolical John Claggart (initials J. C.!), were sympathetically drawn, but they remain secondary characters. Two American tragedies offer Satans as chief characters. We must account for Joe Christmas in Faulkner's *Light in August,* a black rapist and murderer whose name and life in significant ways echo Jesus Christ's. And we must account for Melville's outrageous introduction of Captain Ahab in *Moby-Dick,* the monomaniacal, devil-worshiping protagonist with a "crucifixion in his face." These characters are not mere parodies of the God of the Christians. They represent a serious view of life formed by the impact of Christianity and American democracy.

Besides Jesus and Adam, Satan is a third tragic Christ. Like Jesus, he is a son of God who is preordained to suffering and catastrophe. Like Adam, he possesses a flaw of character that God predestined and used as the instrument of his fall. Satan becomes another channel for God's inscrutable purpose regarding men. He is not merely an antagonist to the Lord, he is His servant, and his sinfulness fulfills God's moral purpose.

Milton's humanization of Satan preserves him from being a theological puppet. He endows the character with human feelings, courage, power, intuition, and sympathy. The tragedy of *Paradise Lost* is shared by a soiled good man (in the Aristotelian tradition) and a steadfast villain (a result of Satan's paradoxical role in Christian theology). In egalitarian tragedy, the common denominator that makes heroes of both Adams and Satans is what Dr. Percival, Sherwood Anderson's philosopher of *Winesburg, Ohio*, taught young George Willard: "The idea is very simple, so simple that if you are not careful you will forget it. It is this—that everyone in the world is Christ and they are all crucified." [1] This statement summarizes the tragic theology of America and prepares the ground for the emergence of Satans who are Christs and Adams.

The ultimate logic is to coalesce these figures into one personality. The paradoxical role that Christianity ascribes to Satan as at once the enemy of God and His servant is reflected in Captain Ahab and Joe Christmas. Both are mania-beset monsters that destroy themselves and others. By all rights of human justice, they should be hateful characters, condemned unpityingly for their monstrosities. But their magnitude and our sympathy for them are derivations from the Christian cosmic scheme. Far from believing in an Armageddon of God or Christ fighting the devil, American tragedians have beaten theological swords into plowshares.

How did Melville and Faulkner do so? The question can be formidable. Aristotle said that the downfall of villains served to feed only the moral sense, certainly not a catharsis of pity and terror. And Ahab and Joe Christmas are noth-

1. Sherwood Anderson, *Winesburg, Ohio*, ed. John H. Ferres (1919; reprint, New York: Viking, 1966), 55–56.

ing if not ostensible villains. One past tragedian that everyone read offered lessons on how to transform diabolical characters into channels of pity and terror. He is William Shakespeare and his exemplary drama of satanic tragedy is *Macbeth*.

SHAKESPEARE'S ANTIHERO

Between the Greeks and Shakespeare there exists, as far as American tragedy is concerned, a hiatus of two thousand years in the literary legacy. During these two millennia, there was, of course, Seneca, but he is either dismissed entirely as a purveyor of degenerate bombast in the mask of tragedy or tolerated merely as a source and inspiration for some Elizabethan plays. Fellow Elizabethans, Christopher Marlowe, John Webster, Francis Beaumont and John Fletcher, John Ford *et al.*, may be beloved by historians of the drama and by aficionados of esoteric modern theatrical productions, but as a body of influence they are not important. Only Shakespeare emerges as the one Elizabethan playwright who demands our attention.

That is not to say that modern tragedians strive to make tragedies as Shakespeare made them. In a certain sense, as William Archer points out, Shakespeare is actually foreign to us. Elizabethan drama portrays no idea of progress, which is the central idea of modern times, especially in America; it portrays a world dependent upon the strictures of a static, stratified, monarchal society—far different from the American ideal; it displays no social consciousness, which is today almost a criminal attitude.[2] It is, from a historical point of view, no surprise that a belief in divine monarchy is reflected in a father-image king on the Elizabethan stage, that an upset in the political corpus can be reflected in trepida-

2. William Archer, *The Old Drama and the New* (Boston: Small, Maynard, 1923), 125, 128.

tions in nature itself, that the state shudders when the hero undergoes his catastrophe. For all their universality, Shakespeare's tragedies arose out of the society of his time.

Herman Melville, however, epitomized what Shakespeare meant to those who were to write tragedies in America. We have already read, in connection with Melville's insights into Hawthorne's tragic vision, the passage in the review of *Mosses from an Old Manse* in which Melville compares the fabulist of Concord to the tragedian of London. Now let us reverse our perspective to see that Melville actually assimilates Shakespeare's tragic vision into the American mainstream. Of Hawthorne, Melville writes: "Certain it is . . . that this great power of blackness in him derives its force from its appeals to that Calvinistic sense of Innate Depravity and Original Sin, from whose visitations in some shape or other, no deeply thinking mind is always and wholly free. . . . It is that blackness in Hawthorne, of which I have spoken, that so fixes and fascinates me." At this point, Melville allies Hawthorne's Calvinistic predilection to

> those deep far-away things in [Shakespeare]; those occasional flashings-forth of the intuitive Truth in him; those short, quick probings at the very axis of reality;—these are the things that make Shakespeare, Shakespeare. Through the mouths of the dark characters of Hamlet, Timon, Lear, and Iago, he craftily says, or sometimes insinuates, the things which we feel to be so terrifically true, that it were all but madness for any good man, in his own proper character, to utter, or even hint of them. Tormented into desperation, Lear, the frantic king, tears off the mask and speaks the same madness of vital truth.[3]

3. Herman Melville, "Hawthorne and His Mosses," in Willard Thorp (ed.), *Herman Melville: Representative Selections* (New York: American Book Co., 1938), 333, 334.

Indeed, Caroline Spurgeon sounds like a critic of the literature of Calvinist New England, rather than of Elizabethan tragedy, when she asserts that the tragedy of *Hamlet*, for example, is *"not as the problem of an individual at all*, but as something greater and more mysterious, as a *condition* for which, the individual himself is apparently not responsible . . . but which, nevertheless, in its course and development, impartially and relentlessly annihilates him and others, innocent and guilty alike." [4] That the great A. C. Bradley avoided this facet of Shakespeare's tragic vision drove Lily Campbell to remonstrate, "The Elizabethans . . . certainly did not have Bradley's hesitation about mentioning God. . . . I can see nothing peculiar about a religious tone produced by the realization in the plot of a play that God is at work in human affairs. . . . I cannot see why Shakespeare did *not* imagine the supreme power as a divine being or as a providence, which supernaturally interferes." [5]

Melville had detected not only the "Calvinistic" character of Shakespeare's blackness—so much a part of Melville's national tradition—but a kind of democracy of blackness as well. Shakespeare's greatest heroes and blackest villains are all caught up in tragic enactments. Elder Olson elaborates upon what Melville caught in Shakespeare's tragic vision: "Shakespeare has worked out his own formula for the tragic *hamartia*, the tragic mistake; and so far as I know, it is one peculiar to him. . . . A character of conspicuous virtues and abilities, who has distinguished himself through them in one sphere, is thrown suddenly into a sphere of action in

---

4. Quoted by Francis Fergusson, *Idea of a Theater* (1949; reprint, New York: Anchor Books, 1953), 145–46; italics are Prof. Spurgeon's own.
5. Lily B. Campbell, *Shakespeare's Tragic Heroes* (1930; reprint, London: Methuen-University Paperbacks, 1961), 264.

which to exercise them—and he *must* exercise them—is to invoke catastrophe. A far sadder notion than the Greek: we fall, not through our vices merely, but even through our virtues." [6]

Shakespeare's concept of tragic heroism, however, is even more ironic: there are heroes who fall through their virtues, but others who rise through their villainy. Shakespeare has passive protagonists, whom John Gassner calls "anti-heroic figures," like Hamlet.[7] He also has protagonists, like Macbeth, who live by the principle of active villainy, whom Herbert Muller calls "morally evil figures," yet who nevertheless exhibit "the terrible possibilities of the human spirit [culminating in a] greatness beyond good and evil." [8] How much more antiheroic are these satanic heroes! Yet in the portrayal of Macbeth, Shakespeare left a legacy to American tragedy of how to transform a fiend into a tragic hero who can arouse not only terror, but pity as well.

There are four stages in this evolution. To begin with, the character first must be established as virtuous; a reservoir of goodwill must be created. When we meet Macbeth in Act I, he is a shrewd and courageous soldier beloved by king and peer. By self-confidence and self-reliance, he has carved out a status of eminence and admiration for himself. He had to work for it and to use strength and ingenuity to rise to that point where the king is anxious to bestow on him the rewards he deserves. Macbeth is also ambitious, a trait without which he could not achieve what he did, but

6. Elder Olson, *Tragedy and the Theory of Drama* (Detroit: Wayne State University Press, 1966), 202.

7. John Gassner, "Possibilities and Perils of Modern Tragedy," in Robert W. Corrigan (ed.), *The Theater in the Twentieth Century* (New York: Grove Press, 1965), 221.

8. Herbert J. Muller, *The Spirit of Tragedy* (1956; reprint, New York: Washington Square Press, 1965), 17.

which as yet has not become the cancer that destroys his good qualities.

The second stage presages the rising villainy, but in an ironic way: the virtues of courage and ambition become the flaws in his character. The witches (whatever aspect of cosmic or psychological fate they represent) know that courage and ambition are the chinks in Macbeth's armor of virtue. These traits which once achieved eminence and respect now work to destroy him. The great soldier becomes a diabolical fiend, killing an old man under his roof, an enormity from the days of the childhood of the race; he has his best friend murdered; he has a woman and a child slain, crimes that always twist the heart of an audience. And yet, August Wilhelm von Schlegel is able to say that Macbeth is, "an ambitious but noble hero, yielding to a deep-laid hellish temptation, [committing crimes] impelled by necessity." [9] Schlegel's interpretation precisely describes the way Satan is understood in American tragic thought—a hellish being impelled by necessity.

It would almost seem that Shakespeare was experimenting with how far he might elasticize Aristotle's dictum that the tragic hero cannot be eminently villainous. Almost at the point of no return Shakespeare begins to rescue the fiend in the sympathy of his audience. Stage three, the transformation of a particular demon into a universal figure, begins. Macbeth's whole world begins to shatter about his head—Birnam wood comes to Dunsinane in ironical fulfillment of the witches' prediction. Here is Macbeth's first opportunity "to walk away," but, of course, Shakespeare cannot have it so. Macbeth once was a great soldier, and so,

9. Quoted by John Dover Wilson (ed.), in "Introduction," *The New Shakespeare: Macbeth* (Cambridge, England, 1968), l. References to the play will be to this edition.

when he hears of the forest lurching toward his castle, he
fulfills this level of his heroic nature:

> I'll fight, till from my bones my flesh be hacked.
> Give me my armour. (V, iii, 33–34)

> Blow, wind! come, wrack!
> At least we'll die with harness on our back.
> (V, v, 51–52)

Shakespeare's rescue operation becomes more dramatic
when Lady Macbeth dies in the throes of a retributive madness that Macbeth knows he is responsible for. With a desperation arising as much from his condition as from his
wife's, he asks the doctor a query he really knows the answer to:

> MACBETH: Canst thou not minister to a mind
>   diseased,
>   Pluck from the memory a rooted sorrow,
>   Raze out the written troubles of the
>   brain
>   And with some sweet oblivious antidote
>   Cleanse the stuffed bosom of that
>   perilous stuff
>   Which weighs upon the heart?
> DOCTOR: Therein, the patient
>   Must minister to himself. (V, iii, 40–46)

The moment of crisis in the character of the hero is at
hand. The climactic stage of transformation reveals the
ability of the heretofore demonic protagonist to experience
anagnorisis. The death of Lady Macbeth is the cue for all
the violent action to stop. A still moment descends upon
the scene. It is a point of dramaturgy that will be remembered in American tragedy. The moment of quiet reflection helps manage the metamorphosis of our reaction from
possible repulsion to probable sympathy. It may not be the
recognition scene of Aristotle's *Poetics* (I suppose Macbeth's

confrontation with Macduff is that); but certainly it is the hero's moment of anagnorisis, the change from ignorance to knowledge. In the "Tomorrow" speech, the hero sees deeply into the real meaning of his petty usurpation, blundering crimes, and silly power. Macbeth expresses for us our unspoken fears about the finitude and foolishness of man and the inevitability of life.

The quiet is soon blasted, and we are drawn by some magnet of ineluctability to the famous confrontation. When he learns that Macduff was of no woman born, Macbeth again might have just walked away. Indeed, Macduff in effect asks him whether this is what he will do. We would not, I think, blame him, shocked as we are by this final irony. For we realize that Macbeth has been a plaything of the gods—the witches' predictions were all along cosmic jokes played on an unsuspecting mortal. But Macbeth, realizing what has been done to his dignity as a man, bows to his fate like a soldier, not like a cringing coward. Shakespeare recalls the Macbeth of Act I and draws upon the reservoir of sympathy he deposited then to secure our pity for his hero in this final stage of transformation. All the threads he has spun out are drawn together: original virtue, the fall because of necessity, the pitiful anagnorisis. The monster becomes Everyman, defeated but victorious. With tacit knowledge that the moral universe prevails, we feel the catharsis.

"However much we may abhor [Macbeth's] actions," said Schlegel, "we cannot altogether refuse to compassionate the state of his mind; we lament the ruin of so many noble qualities." [10] Macbeth, we realize, was chosen, in Shakespeare's world picture because of his heroic nature, and his creator, avers Dover Wilson, "succeeds in endowing

10. *Ibid.*

the 'tyrant bloody-sceptred' with enough nobility and 'human kindness' to claim our pity." [11]

And terror? James Joyce taught us that terror comes from the recognition that there is a dark and secret cause, some superpowerful Other out there in the palpable obscure. Writes Dover Wilson: "Macbeth's heaven-defying fury . . . shows him as a rebel against fate, against the whole 'estate o' the world,' against 'both the worlds,' natural and supernatural; a rebel refusing to recognize defeat and fighting his last and hopeless battle with growing despair but undiminished resolution." [12]

In full knowledge that Macbeth, this satanic antihero, is a bloody criminal of the worst sort, the catharsis that Shakespeare arouses forces us to set aside our standard notions of right and wrong. In no way does the author permit us the luxury of the thought that Macbeth got what he deserved: "Morality," the critic Walter Raleigh said, "is not denied; it is overwhelmed . . . [by the realization that] at any moment by the operation of chance, or fate, [civilization] may be broken up, and the world given over once more to the forces that struggled in chaos." [13]

Shakespeare re-formed in drama the ancient ideological problems of Judeo-Christian thinking about Satan that heretofore were confined to the Bible and a biblical epic. But more: Shakespeare demonstrates the way to resurrect our goodwill toward the antihero—emphasize his essential humanity. He turns our attention away from the rapaciousness of Macbeth's nature through the foil of his love for Lady Macbeth; through the recollection at the end of Macbeth's admirable qualities displayed at the beginning; through dramatizing the perplexity in Macbeth's and all our hearts, when we face the cracking of our little worlds. Thus Shakespeare leaves us to witness in awe and pity the

11. *Ibid.,* xiv.   12. *Ibid.,* lxv.   13. Quoted *ibid.,* lxvii.

humanity of this hero. If American writers have not equaled his creative powers, they have, in two satanic tragedies, *Moby-Dick* and *Light in August*, reached his highest humanism.

IN NOMINE DIABOLI

Forty years before he wrote *Billy Budd*, Herman Melville was in no mood for testaments of Christological resignation. In February, 1849, he had begun to read Shakespeare's later tragedies;[14] on the flyleaf of one volume he wrote an impious dedication to Satan and a few lines on madness.[15] In late October, while once again on the high seas voyaging to the Continent, he records in his journal a recollection of Milton's *Paradise Lost*: "walked the deck with the German, Mr. Adler till a late hour, talking of 'Fixed Fate, Free will, fore-knowledge absolute,' "[16] the very topic discussed by the fallen angels in Book 2, line 500. Back home by February, 1850, Melville begins *Moby-Dick* as a sea adventure in the manner of his earlier novels; Queequeg and Ishmael apparently are his comic heroes.[17] A month later he reads and underscores in a new Bible a number of dark passages in Ecclesiastes and the Book of Job. In August when the book, he claims, was "mostly done," he reads Hawthorne's *Mosses from an Old Manse* and writes his famous review.[18]

Shakespeare, Milton, Job, and Hawthorne. When *Moby-Dick* was finally published in October/November of 1851, this combination of tragedy and dark symbolism had pushed Queequeg into a minor role in the story, transformed Ish-

14. Jay Leyda, *The Melville Log* (New York: Harcourt, Brace, 1951), 288.
15. Lawrance Thompson, *Melville's Quarrel with God* (Princeton, N.J.: Princeton University Press, 1952), 137.
16. Leyda, *The Melville Log*, 319.
17. George R. Stewart, "The Two Moby-Dicks," *American Literature*, XXIV (1954), 418.
18. Leyda, *The Melville Log*, 369, 385, 388.

mael into the book's narrator, and coagulated Melville's
restless vision into the figure of Captain Ahab, a tragic hero
who forevermore holds the center stage of the book.

Tucked into Melville's first physical description of this
fierce old man is the physical symbol of Ahab's satanic
origin:

> Threading its way out from among his grey hairs, and con-
> tinuing right down one side of his tawny scorched face and
> neck, till it disappeared in his clothing, you saw a slender
> rod-like mark, lividly whitish. It resembled that perpendic-
> ular seam sometimes made in the straight, lofty trunk of a
> great tree, when the upper lightning tearingly darts down
> it . . . leaving the tree still greenly dark, but branded.
> Whether that mark was born into him, or whether it was the
> scar left by some desperate wound, no one could say. (Chap-
> ter 28, pp. 120–21)[19]

Clearly, Ahab, as many have noticed for a long time, wears
the mask of Satan.

The most striking characteristic of Captain Ahab is his
rebelliousness, which is his form of hubris. It is literarily
derived from two titanic superhuman rebels. Melville calls
Ahab a Promethean (Chapter 44, p. 200) and endows him
with an intermittent Miltonic satanism. Both of these characters are theological criminals, both are superlative tyrannoi who see their world in their own design and then
against all cosmic power and justice go about measuring it
out by their ingenuity and bravery.

But these figures are demigods, battling out their heroism on a cosmic plane. Terrestrial tragic heroes, like Oedipus and Macbeth, all ultimately bow before the power of
the Omnipotent Other. Only Captain Ahab, among human

---

19. Herman Melville, *Moby-Dick, or The Whale*, ed. Luther Mansfield
and H. P. Vincent (Centenary ed.; New York: Hendricks House, 1952). Page
references in the text are to this edition. For the convenience of readers
with other editions, chapters are also cited.

heroes, retains a transcendent hubris beyond the pale of
normal tragic heroism and cries out to the corposants, the
fiery symbols of his god, "Defyingly, I worship thee!" So ex-
treme is his defiance that, when he is dead and no longer
even aboard the *Pequod,* his ship in its final plunge carries
with it a live part of God's nature. For such a hero, only
the name Ahab is appropriate—"Ahab, [who] did more to
provoke the Lord God of Israel than all the kings of Israel
that were before him" (1 Kings 16:33). We have to go back
to the provocation of Satan, in Christian lore and Milton's
epic, to find its equal. No wonder Melville crowed to Hawthorne that he had written "a wicked book" and dedicated
it secretly to Satan.[20]

Truly there are innumerable incidents of flamboyant defiance, human isolation, and black worship strewn throughout the book, climaxed by a scene from a witches' Sabbath
in which Ahab dedicates the harpoon that will search for
Moby-Dick's heart: "Three punctures were made in the
heathen flesh [of the three harpooneers], and the White
Whale's barbs were then tempered. 'Ego non baptizo te in
nomine patris, sed in nomine diaboli!' deliriously howled
Ahab, as the malignant iron scorchingly devoured his bap-
tismal blood" (Chapter 113, p. 484). The almost identical
devil's oath that Melville had written onto the flyleaf of his
copy of Shakespeare defied not only "nomine patris," the
name of the Father, but also "et Filii et Spiritus Sancti,"
the Son and the Holy Spirit. I suggest that there is some
significance in the change that canceled the mention of
Christ and the Holy Ghost.

Melville played a bit boyish in those letters to Hawthorne. The man who saved a place for Chillingworth near

20. Melville to Hawthorne, in M. R. Davis and W. H. Gilman (eds.),
Letters of Herman Melville (New Haven: Yale University Press, 1960), 133,
142.

the throne of the Heavenly King would certainly see through Melville's exhilaration and perceive underneath the same equilibrium of tragedy that ballasted his own diabolic creation. As satanic as Melville wanted to seem in his letters, in his book he did not try to escape the demands of Christian tragedy that saw in Satan a career of moral villainy fulfilling a purpose of moral necessity. The satanism of Ahab is never complete and never stands alone. Always Melville softens it even as he presents it. In the same paragraph that he describes the scorched face of the captain, Melville writes: "Moody stricken Ahab stood before [the crew] with a crucifixion in his face; in all the nameless regal overbearing dignity of some mighty woe" (Chapter 28, p. 122). In American tragedy, the mask of Christ may by itself adorn the face of a tragic hero, but the mask of Satan must reveal concomitant lineaments of Christ.

From this early point on, Melville clothes his satanic hero with the Christological mystique. Ahab, too, is a Man of Sorrows. The mighty woe visited upon him stems from the same source of tragic destiny that enveloped Christ. Ahab, the most defiant hero, is brother to Jesus, the most submissive one. To make us imagine Ahab with a crucifixion in his face allays the dark diabolism of his conduct and prepares us to understand his closeness to another Christological hero, that of the Book of Job, who also was given over to the hands of Satan.

Melville fashioned his book, say the editors of the Centenary edition, "as a kind of nineteenth century Book of Job." [21] In *Moby-Dick*, wrote Odell Shepard, "not so much the actual words and tales of the Bible, but its inmost spirit and essence, its grandeur and its tragedy, have passed into the mind of Melville. His Ahab is a modern Job with Job's huge, insoluble problem tormenting heart and brain, and

21. Melville, *Moby-Dick*, 640.

with Job's large utterance." [22] Ahab, too, had his comforters, members of the crew with conventional advice. One after another, they approach him—Stubb, Pip, finally Starbuck. Starbuck sees blasphemy in Ahab's mission: "Vengeance on a dumb brute! . . . to be enraged with a dumb thing, Captain Ahab, seems blasphemous" (Chapter 36, p. 161). Ahab, replying as Job replied to his friends, feels his partnership in the tragic covenant and places the matter in proper perspective: "How can the prisoner reach outside except by thrusting through the wall? To me, the white whale is that wall shoved near to me. Sometimes I think there's naught beyond. But 'tis enough. He tasks me; he heaps me, I see in him outrageous strength, with an inscrutable malice sinewing it. That inscrutable thing is chiefly what I hate; and be the white whale agent, or be the white whale principal, I will wreak that hate upon him" (Chapter 36, p. 162).

This speech may be impious, but it is not apostate. Job did not question the justice in the seeming malice of God, nor does Ahab. Job did not challenge the might of God, nor does Ahab. Months later, in the midst of an electrical storm, with the yardarms alight with the corposants, St. Elmo's fire, Ahab worships: "Thou clear spirit, of thy fire thou madst me, and like a true child of fire, I breathe it back to thee. . . . I own thy speechless, placeless power; said I not so? Nor was it wrung from me; nor so I now drop these links" (Chapter 119, p. 500).

Whether God is symbolized by fire or by the leviathan, it is "that inscrutable thing" that Job and Ahab chiefly

22. Quoted by Carlos Baker, "The Place of the Bible in American Fiction," in James Smith and A. Leland Jamison (eds.), *Religion in American Life* (4 vols.; Princeton, N.J.: Princeton University Press, 1961), II, 262–63, n. 32. See also Richard B. Sewall, *Vision of Tragedy* (New Haven: Yale University Press, 1959), 102, and F. X. Canfield, "*Moby-Dick* and the Book of Job," *Catholic World*, CLXXIV (1952), 254–60.

hate, not the malice. The problem for both is the problem of knowledge. And in the pursuit of it, Ahab, like his forebear, sticks tragically to his integrity. Having had thrust upon him and taken upon himself the quest for truth, the hero, like Job before him, must now "declare himself a sovereign nature . . . amid the power of heaven, hell, and earth," as Melville said elsewhere.[23] In the very accents that Job spoke the verse, "Though he slay me, yet will I trust in him; but I will maintain mine own ways before him" (Job 13:15, a verse which Melville underlined in his Bible in 1850), Ahab cries to the corposants: "Thou canst blind; but I can then grope; Thou canst consume; but I can then be ashes; . . . Yet blindfold, yet will I talk to thee" (Chapter 119, p. 500).

As much God's champion as Job was, Ahab too succeeds in taunting the Almighty out of heaven. God answers Ahab not out of a whirlwind, but in the embodiment of the leviathan with which He had millennia before taunted Job. For three days, Moby-Dick swims away, but then, teased beyond normal provocation, the whale turns, staving in the ship and drowning all hands save one. Ishmael, the survivor, serves as Ahab's disciple, traveling about the earth, telling the tale to future generations. Ahab's catastrophe, then, fulfills the crucifixion in his face that foretold his end. At the last the features of Christ blur the mask of Satan.

No doubt allusions to Christ and Job softened the villainy of the captain in his own Bible-intoxicated generation, but the eternality of Captain Ahab as a tragic figure must rest on more commonplace foundations. He must be shown as a human being caught up, as we are, in the *agon* of fate and individual desire.

Melville's dramatic problem with Ahab is similar to

23. Melville to Hawthorne, April 16(?), 1851, in Davis and Gilman (eds.), *Letters*, 124.

Shakespeare's with Macbeth. How is one to generate sympathy and goodwill for a harsh, satanic protagonist? Shakespeare's ploy was to reveal the basic humanity of the hero and to remind the audience of it every so often. This is Melville's method as well. Even before we meet Captain Ahab, he has Peleg tell Ishmael, "[Ahab] has a wife not three voyages wedded—a sweet, resigned girl. Think of that; by that sweet girl that old man has a child; hold ye then there can be any utter, hopeless harm in Ahab? No, no, my lad; stricken, blasted if he be, Ahab has his humanities" (Chapter 16, p. 80).

Ironically, the violation of these humanities triggers the tragedy, but it is not Ahab's volition that does so. In a sermon ostensibly about Jonah, Father Mapple, the prophet-like preacher in the Seaman's Bethel, unwittingly predicts the disintegration of Ahab's humanity: "And if we obey God we must disobey ourselves; and it is in this disobeying ourselves wherein the hardness of obeying God consists" (Chapter 9, p. 41). The first time Ahab disobeys the calling of natural tendencies is in the quarterdeck scene when he mentally overawes the crew and his mates and forces them to swear to hunt Moby-Dick. Right after, like Macbeth after the murder of Duncan, Ahab soliloquizes upon the shock of realizing what he had done. The tone of his words echoes Macbeth's: "This [the moon's] lovely light, it lights not me; all loveliness is anguish to me, since I ne'er can enjoy . . . Damned, most subtly and most malignantly! damned in the midst of paradise." Quickly, he recovers and concludes defyingly, "Over unsounded gorges, through rifled heats of mountains, under torrents' beds, unerringly I rush! Naught's an obstacle, naught's an angle to the iron way!" (Chapter 37, pp. 165–66).

Ahab, too, separates himself from mankind. His isolation is complete except for Starbuck, and it's Starbuck who creates a Macbethian moment of stillness before Ahab's anagnorisis. Starbuck recalls, together with a momentarily serene Captain Ahab, the balmy days in Nantucket and the wife and boy on the hilltop overlooking the bay. The eyes of the mate and the captain lock for a moment in human kinship, and the whole search for the whale hangs in suspension. Then the total realization of what is demanded of Ahab breaks over him: "What is it, what nameless, inscrutable, unearthly thing is it; what cozzening, hidden lord and master, and cruel, remorseless emperor *commands* me; that against all natural lovings and longings, I so keep pushing, and crowding, and jamming myself on all the time; recklessly making me ready to do what in my own proper, natural heart, I durst not so much as dare? Is Ahab, Ahab? Is it I, God, or who, that lifts this arm?" (Chapter 132, p. 536, my italics). Roiling through our memories come the lines from *Paradise Lost* in which Milton, in the midst of his own humanization of Satan in Book 1, ascribes the fiend's sins to "the will / And high permission of all-ruling Heaven" (Book 1, l. 211–12).

The drying up of Ahab's humanities calls to our pity. The interpolation of God's inscrutable will over his natural desires germinates terror. Long before, using in fact the same terminology as Ahab, Father Mapple sermonized upon what Ahab now discovers: "All things that God would have us do are hard for us to do—remember that—and hence, He oftener *commands* than endeavors to persuade" (Chapter 9, p. 41, my italics).

The minister's prophecies are not the only prophecies that strike terror in the soul. Melville borrowed from *Macbeth* the device of impossible predictions that are strangely fulfilled. *Macbeth* has its witches, *Moby-Dick* has Fedallah. Each of the impossibilities that he prophesies must occur before the death of Ahab will occur, and regardless of the demonic character of the protagonist, we are awed by the knowledge his world is breaking apart. Satanic though he is, Ahab is first of all a man: "This august dignity I treat of, is not the dignity of kings and robes, but that abounding dignity which has no robed investiture ... that democratic dignity which, on all hands radiates with out end from God; Himself! ... If, then, to meanest mariners, and renegades and castaways, I shall hereafter ascribe high qualities, though dark; [and] weave round them tragic graces ... bear me out in it, O God!" (Chapter 35, p. 114). A hundred years before Arthur Miller spoke, Herman Melville sounded the tocsin of modern tragedy.

It is a Christian equilibrium and a democratic one. Ahab's satanic sin is without guilt, and his guilt is without sin. He attracts God's attention, plays the game of tragedy, and suffers for it. His self-reliance is the attraction and the goad. He symbolizes the tension between sovereignty and freedom, between the destiny of Christ and the destiny of Satan. We pity Ahab for his suffering, we are awed by the dimensions of his tragedy, but we also take pride in the fact that an American hero dies in defiance of limitation.

BLACK EASTER

When we turn to consider William Faulkner's tragic hero, Joe Christmas, in *Light in August* (1932), we reach a climax in the history of American tragic writing. His demonism is even more horrific than Captain Ahab's. Yet Faulkner endows him with every phase of tragic heroism from divine morality to satanic criminality. The tragic masks Joe Christmas wears reveal his ancestry, too, as not only Satan and Macbeth, but Oedipus and Jesus.

The setting of *Light in August* is the South, and in the three interrelated stories that compose the book, various phases of this particular mystique are operative. In the story of Lena Grove, the mythic earth-naturalism of the southern countryside is depicted. In the story of Gail Hightower, the potent memory of the single dominating fact of the southern past, the Civil War, is invoked. In the story of Joe Christmas, the single most dominating fact of the southern past and present, the specter of race, propels the action of the tragedy.

Faulkner compounds the complexity of telling three stories simultaneously by the use of flashback in each of the narrative strands. Of these, Lena's past is most simple, Gail Hightower's most sentimental, and Joe's most dramatic, most complicated, most mysterious, and most tragic. This element in the structure of the book needs a bit of explication, because Faulkner uses it as a means to reach a catharsis in Joe's tragedy.

The first time we hear of Joe Christmas, he is already thirty years old and is on the run from the law. He is accused of murdering his middle-aged white do-gooder mistress, Joanna Burden, and of setting the torch to her mansion. The first mark that Joe wears, then, in the narrative time sequence of *Light in August* is Satan's, just as it was the mark of Faulkner's tyrannos, Thomas Sutpen. Then, flashback forces us to reorder our conception of the hero. We never forget the satanic posture of the protagonist, but remembrances of his past—his childhood, youth, courage, persistence—compel us to moderate our emotional response to him. In the case of Joe Christmas, this reordering of our reactions begins with Christological allusions, as his story is told by his grandfather who loves/hates him.

To be born illegitimately on Christmas morn in the equivalent of a manger is a big joke that augurs either a parallelism of Christological saintliness or plumb line to satanic depravity. It is Faulkner's sardonic tragic sense to name him after the Savior and make him a fiend. Rejected by his grandparents after his mother dies and his Mexican or white or Negro father disappears, Joe spends a few inno-cent years in an orphan asylum. He falls from this inno-cence, symbolically, when he accidentally witnesses the coitus of a doctor and a nurse—the act that drove Adam and Eve out of Paradise. After a time, he is adopted by a child-less fundamentalist couple. Joe is introduced to a dour Christianity quite opposite Jesus' religion of love. He re-bels, runs away, and begins a fifteen-year search for identity. Is he white or is he black?

The road he travels includes nearly every detour into depravity one can think of—low women, crime, bestiality to white and black. He travels in the North and finds no surcease, so he returns to the South. He falls in with a north-ern woman driven by white guilt feelings and unrequited sexual desire. After a mad love affair which includes per-version and prayer, he slits her throat. Then he escapes. During his flight, his frustration reaches an apex of erup-tion when he bursts into a Negro revivalist church meeting and drives all the worshipers out. Here his mask is recog-nized: one of the Negroes cries out, "It's the devil! It's Sa-tan himself!" (282)[24]

The very irony of the gap between allusion and perfor-mance nurtures our response of pity and terror. The ancient Christ, who bears the perfection of heaven and assumes the curse of mankind, is balanced by the modern, aberrated Christmas, who symbolizes the depravity of self as the orig-inal condition of mankind. It is the scheme of things that both lurch toward a crucifixion to be reborn. Eminent vir-tue and eminent depravity alike, in modern, democratic tragedy, can be synthesized into a tragic enactment.

In the American South, it is, of course, vital to know if

24. William Faulkner, *Light in August* (1932; reprint, New York: Modern Library, 1950). Page references are incorporated in the text in parentheses.

one's father had only darkish skin or black man's blood. But Joe Christmas transcends this regional circumstance to become an Everyman searching for a self. One immediately recalls Sophocles' tragic drama on the same theme, and grafting Oedipus onto the characterization of Joe Christmas is no introduction of a foreign body.

Faulkner can graft Oedipus Tyrannos onto a hero who bears the features of Satan and Christ, because Oedipus, too, was fated and crucified. John Longley has described the similarities of both these protagonists:[25] both are foundlings, both prosecute a search for identity, both reject alternatives that would sway them from this search. For both the vital classical question of fate and choice hangs like a cloud over the peripety. Though we knew he was fated, Oedipus always thought he knew who he was, and his search for identity was ostensibly accidental. His journey to realization is no pilgrimage to reach a prechosen goal. He does not know, until the moment the gods turn up the ace in their cosmic game, that the unwitting wandering toward truth had been all along a purposeful journey. The amount of fate in the scale of Oedipus' choice is overwhelming. Joe Christmas always knew that he did not know who and what he was, and to him this was an overwhelming question. He seems to make a conscious choice to follow a road that perhaps will lead to the answer. Yet it is impossible to determine what is fate and what is choice. In keeping with modern psychological insights, one reader has said that "Christmas is not *determined* by his past; he *is* the past. . . . It is in his consciousness that we must seek his feeling of being dominated by destiny [because] destiny is in fact an inner force."[26] Thus Faulkner augments the

25. John Longley, "Joe Christmas: The Hero in the Modern World," in Frederick J. Hoffman and Olga Vickery (eds.), *William Faulkner: Three Decades of Criticism* (Lansing: University of Michigan Press, 1960), 269–70.
26. Jean Pouillon. "Time and Destiny in Faulkner," trans. J. Merrians,

reservoir of pity and terror that he will presently draw upon.

Now Faulkner faces a dramatic problem that the ancient tragedian did not. When Sophocles picks up the story of Oedipus, all of his hero's violence is behind him, and the passion we witness is the passion of pride. When Faulkner picks up the story of Christmas all of his hero's violence is in one sense behind him, but we are not let off the hook. Through flashback and memory we are forced to witness the violence of mindless anger in all the horrific depth and detail that this Gothic-minded author can plumb. If Joe Christmas had ever initially touched the wellsprings of our pity, in the middle part of the book he grows into a repulsive grotesque.

The methodology of *Macbeth*, the tragedy of another repulsive grotesque, saves him for the catharsis. The same progression of plot and development of character that served Shakespeare in that drama serves Faulkner in *Light in August*. Our first glimpse of Macbeth is of a great soldier, resolute, courageous, admirable, and yet human. As an audience we are ready to identify with him. In his reconstruction of Joe Christmas' life, Faulkner uses the innocent childhood of his hero to create in us a positive response to him. It is a cynical adult world that destroys Joe's innocence and fashions his future choices of actions. Thus, as Oscar Mandel said of him, "[He is] stunted before [he] can begin life on [his] own. We pity [him], we cry out against the world."

But, Mandel adds, Joe Christmas "do[es] not obtain our good will." [27] Did Macbeth, in that period of the play in which he commits enormities? Yet, attempting to tease early sympathy into lasting goodwill, Shakespeare allows us

in Robert Penn Warren (ed.), *William Faulkner: A Collection of Critical Essays* (Englewood Cliffs, N.J.: Prentice-Hall, 1966), 84.

27. Oscar Mandel, *A Definition of Tragedy* (New York: New York University Press, 1961), 105.

to wonder: who speaks when the witches call to Macbeth—
fate or his own will? And once Macbeth shows his nature as
a tyrannos, how much of fate mockingly forces him into a
policy of murder to solidify his throne? Similarly, to achieve
catharsis, Faulkner balances the pity created for the young
Joe Christmas with the terror he makes us perceive through
a doubt about Joe's responsibility for his evil deeds. The
driven antihero refuses love, rejects the Christianity of both
black and white men, but desperately saves his pride—
through a foul and bloody murder. Yet for all his mon-
strousness, Joe Christmas beats and kills only when his self-
respect is threatened, as when his foster father McEachern
and his mistress Joanna Burden want him to knuckle under
to a totalitarian Christianity. When, however, on the fateful night of the murder, he is picked up by a young couple
who do *not* threaten him, he does not kill them, though he
knows they could recognize him. They do not tamper with
his pride.

His search for self-respect is laudable, but the pride that
motivates him to look for it becomes, like Macbeth's ambition, cancerous. It consumes almost all the goodness and
balance in him, but like Macbeth, he reveals a steely center
of dignity. He retains our regard, so that against all logic,
when his world crumbles, as Macbeth's at Dunsinane, we
still pity him, and a small voice of terror in us asks, How
far different are the righteous and the depraved heroes in
the destiny that overtakes them?

In time, there comes for Joe Christmas the moment of
light and quiet that served Macbeth so well in commending
himself once more to his audience's favor. First there is
the pause in the relentless hurtling of action: "[Joe] paused
... only long enough to lace up the brogans, the black shoes,
the black shoes smelling of negro. . . . It seemed to him that

he could see himself being hunted by white men at last into the black abyss which had been waiting, trying for thirty years to drown him and into which now and at last he had actually entered" (313). Thus he makes his commitment. His anagnorisis, the light that dawns in August, emphasizes the climax and the equilibrium he now experiences:

> It is just dawn, daylight: that gray and lonely suspension filled with the peaceful and tentative waking of birds. . . . He breathes deep and slow, feeling with each breath himself diffuse in the neutral grayness, becoming one with loneliness and quiet that has never known fury or despair. "That was all I wanted," he thinks in a quiet and slow amazement. "That was all, for thirty years. That didn't seem to be a whole lot to ask in thirty years." (289)

He settles for the completion of his destiny, not for victory, for victory is never available to tragic heroes, be they tyrannoi, or Satans, or Christs. The last words of his anagnorisis recognize the interplay of choice and fate and echo Macbeth's tomorrows and yesterdays. " 'I have been farther in these seven days than in all the thirty years,' he thinks, 'But I have never got outside that circle. I have never broken out of the ring of what I have already done and cannot ever undo' " (296). He turns his face to Mottstown, as Jesus turned to Jerusalem, for then could the Scripture be fulfilled, as the Gospel says.

Structurally, Faulkner now does what Shakespeare did in *Macbeth* to ensure the catharsis: he reverses the cycle of the hero's life. With the introduction of an omnipotent "Player" late in the novel we turn back from the climax of Macbethian antiheroism to the fatalism of Oedipus and Christ.

At the same time the Player is invoked, Percy Grimm enters the story. Grimm organizes a vigilante posse, and becomes Christmas' nemesis. The process leading to Christmas' catastrophe is likened by Faulkner to "the implacable undeviation of Juggernaut or Fate" (403). Everything seems to fall into a preconceived plan authored above somewhere: "[Grimm] was moving again almost before he had stopped, with the lean, swift, blind obedience to whatever Player moved him on the Board" (405). When Joe escapes from the sheriff, Grimm and his posse discover him. He cannot escape them. He runs into Gail Hightower's house. Although the deputy sheriff's car is positioned "just where the Player had devised it to be" (405), it is fated that Percy Grimm and his modern Roman garrison and no one else shall kill Joe Christmas: "It was as though [Grimm] had been merely waiting for the Player to move him again, because with that unfailing certitude he ran straight to the kitchen and into the doorway already firing" (406).

Now Faulkner reprises the Christological nature of his hero, that which marked him at his very birth. Born a Christ, he must die like one. Mortally wounded, Joe is not left to die: "The Player was not done yet." One more scene had to be played. Joe lies on the kitchen floor; around him stand his tormentors, like Roman soldiers. Percy Grimm takes a kitchen knife, and in an obscene reenactment of piercing the side of Jesus Christ, castrates Joe Christmas. The blood gushes out. "Upon that black blast the man seemed to rise soaring into their memories forever and ever. They are not to lose it, in whatever peaceful valleys. . . . It will be there, musing, quiet, steadfast, not fading and not particularly threatful, but of itself alone triumphant" (407). Transformed at last from a Satan to a Christ, the tragedy of Joe Christmas concludes with a scene of didactic catastrophe.

The ascension of Joe Christmas is not his own alone. He embodies the characteristics of all American tragic heroes —the tyrannoi and antiheroes, the eloquent and the inarticulate, and he carries them upward with him into the Valhalla of tragic heroism where all the world's tragic heroes are enshrined. What Faulkner said of him and his legacy can be said of the tragic heroes of American literature and their legacy: They "will be there, musing, quiet, steadfast, not fading and not particularly threatful, but of themselves alone triumphant." Equilibrium is all.

Epilogue

As this book goes to press in November, 1973, the arts in America are just beginning, it would seem, to scramble out of the slough of despond that they have been wallowing in for nearly twenty years. This nadir of the spirit has been reflected in literary art of the theater of the absurd, a form of black comedy in which life gets you coming and going, and by fiction and films of solipsistic rebellion against history and decency. The insistence upon immediacy as the only knowledge worth anyone's while resulted in the primacy of brutalized sexuality and indiscriminate violence in works of the imagination.

Such "realism" and "truths" were characteristic of Stanley Kubrick's film *A Clockwork Orange*, in which not one member of the dramatis personae retains a shred of humanity or dignity. This is a preachment of human depravity that would have horrified the most Calvinistic of New England ministers. The same degradation of the human being can be perceived in Philip Roth's *Portnoy's Complaint*, where, behind the facade of adolescent humor, the author has his protagonist destroy his familial past and present relationships. We must wait for the last line of the book —Portnoy is about to begin the major part of his therapy— for any indication of hope, and even that is based upon the fashionable panacea of psychoanalysis.

On the other hand, in a novel published nearly simul-

169

taneously, *Herzog*, Saul Bellow lifted his voice against such purveyors of desperate pessimism and branded them mockingly as "reality instructors" who actually falsified reality. That is the note that is being heard more and more. The pendulum has just begun to swing the other way. Without sugaring the truth of life, literature is softening its rejection of the past. It is a way of admitting that the present was once the past's future.

I like to think that tragedy, the highest form of literature that bespeaks both hard reality and stubborn hope, has had something to do with this redemption of the arts. The significance of the persistence of tragedy in commercial theater and film has been underestimated as an expression of the mood and mind of the audience. Sophocles and Euripides, kept alive recently only in university theater departments, have been called back to Broadway. Last season, new films of *King Lear* and *Macbeth* were shown simultaneously. These are all commercial ventures. There's money in tragedy, because audiences appreciate the rise of human dignity out of the fires of violence. Current literature does not depict this phoenixlike quality that is the hallmark of classical and Elizabethan tragedy.

Alongside these classics, American tragedy, too, has been revived. Several years ago, Miller's *Death of a Salesman* achieved astounding widespread success as a television presentation. Willy Loman became everyone's Everyman; his tragedy has been clearly cathartic. Tennessee Williams' *A Streetcar Named Desire* is about to be revived. Amazingly, even O'Neill's tragic trilogy, *Mourning Becomes Electra*, five hours of Greco-American gloom, after gathering dust for decades, received two revivals within two and a half years. In academic circles, Faulkner's two tragedies, *Absalom, Absalom!* and *Light in August*, are challenging his melodramatic experimental tour de force, *The Sound and the Fury,* for most frequent attention. Hard as life is, we no longer want to be left sinking in the quagmire of frustration.

The new literature of violence has shown its rebelliousness against the past by overthrowing standard literary forms. Novels are often nonstories, and plays are often expressionistic sequences of scenes. Aristotle certainly would have been bewildered to learn that an organic plot no longer meets the demands of current reality. But recent tragedy has proved that even Aristotelian form can be liberated without being destroyed. Even here, the past can be useful.

This revival of respect for form signifies a revival of respect for what the past can teach our spirit. Tragedy has led the counterreaction to the nihilism that has become fashionable in recent literary ideology. Nihilism, it must be recognized, degraded Kierkegaard's religious existentialism into a philosophy that denigrates God and man. For a couple of decades the literary expression of this tendency had found favor among fashionable professors and students. Sartre and Camus ruled. American tragedy, however, persistently corrected their vision by teaching the morality of God, even in catastrophe, and the primacy of man, even in his pain. It is a happy irony that, after Auschwitz and Hiroshima, tragedy can exhilarate us with terror, pity, and above all, dignity and hope. This is its highest reach because this is realism of the highest order.

One might point out that this Epilogue is based only on the revival of tragedies, not upon newly written works. New tragedies have not been written for perhaps twenty years now, but in that time (except for the truncated spurt during the days of John Fitzgerald Kennedy) America has been in an emotional descent. History shows that tragedy is not written during periods of decline but during the apex of a society's cycles. It would seem that despair produces melodrama and ebullience produces new tragedy. Equilibrium is all, and until the moment when America needs a new set of correctives, the old ones will have to do. The revival of older works apparently corrects the leaning toward hopelessness; new plays and dramas correct the leaning toward hubris.

If I am right, we are on the verge of new tragic works. Always few in number, they will, however, last long in man's memory. Once again, perhaps, Emerson's hope will be fulfilled for the poet who, with tyrannous eye, will perceive the miraculous in the common. Then once again history will be blended with contemporaneity, morality with liberty, form with theme, and the genealogy of tragic heroism will bear new progeny.

Bibliographical Essay

One of the purposes of this book is to strew throughout the footnotes a bibliography of critical literature on the subject of American tragic writing. Almost all of the footnoted commentary, however, is brief: articles, chapters, even sentences on specific works. The intention of this essay is to direct the reader's attention to a number of works that have been helpful to me in fashioning a cohesive purview of American tragedy. Some are obvious aids and need no elaborate justification for inclusion here. Others, on the other hand, are indirect, even oblique; about these I must necessarily be subjective. No materials exist that directly suggest overall approaches to American tragedy in two genres (play and novel) during one hundred years of practice. Such items, for me, transcended their author's goals and engendered lines of thought they never had in mind. To them, this essay will both express my gratitude and suggest their value to others.

The first indispensable tool is, of course, Aristotle's *Poetics*. Of the myriad editions available, even of S. H. Butcher's translation, the Hill and Wang paperback (New York, 1961) has the added feature of Francis Fergusson's introduction.

Among the many general studies of tragedy, Herbert J. Muller's *The Spirit of Tragedy* (1956; reprint, New York:

Washington Square Press, 1965) is most balanced about the contributions of American drama to the canon of tragedy. For the drama, Elder Olson, *Tragedy and the Theory of Drama* (Detroit: Wayne State University Press, 1961), demonstrates clearly the relationship of form, technique, and tragic vision. Francis Fergusson, *Idea of a Theatre* (1949; reprint, New York: Anchor Books, 1953), and Oscar Mandel, *A Definition of Tragedy* (New York: New York University Press, 1961), are both provocative—a euphemism for saying that one gets ideas from disagreeing with them at times. Though he wrote on *Greek Tragedy* (London: Methuen, 1966), H. D. F. Kitto displayed such wise criticism that one may transfer it, with accommodations of course, to considerations of tragedy in any culture. Richard B. Sewall's *Vision of Tragedy* (New Haven: Yale University Press, 1959) has the distinction of offering chapters on American fiction among those on the classics of the genre, without apology.

Recently there has been a spate of collections of essays and extracted chapters on tragic vision, form, and history. The best are in R. W. Corrigan (ed.), *Tragedy: Vision and Form* (San Francisco: Chandler, 1965) and in Laurence Michel and Richard B. Sewall (eds.), *Tragedy: Modern Essays in Criticism* (Englewood Cliffs, N.J.: Prentice-Hall, 1963). Corrigan is more complete, including selections from ancients and moderns, from theoretical and practical critics, and from tragic writers themselves. Corrigan also has an extensive bibliography. Cleanth Brooks's collection, *Tragic Themes in Western Literature* (1955; reprint, New Haven: Yale University Press, 1960), is simply brilliant. Though no American play or novel made it into its hallowed pages, Bernard Knox's essay, "Sophocles' Oedipus," suggests a major insight into American tragic vision.

Two other books that do not deal with American literature do a similar job: Susanne K. Langer, *Philosophy in a New Key* (New York: Mentor, 1953), and Northrup Frye, *Anatomy of Criticism* (1957; reprint, New York; Atheneum, 1965).

We turn now to American literature itself. Two books on intellectual and social backgrounds form the backdrop, as it were, of American tragedy: Ralph Henry Gabriel, *The Course of American Democratic Thought* (2nd ed.; New York: Ronald, 1956); and Rod W. Horton and Herbert W. Edwards, *Backgrounds of American Literary Thought* (2nd ed.; New York: Appleton-Century-Crofts, 1967). The second edition of the latter book contains an excellent survey of existentialism in the frame of American literature. Randall Stewart, *American Literature and Christian Doctrine* (Baton Rouge: Louisiana State University Press, 1958), and Nathan Scott, *The Tragic Vision and the Christian Faith* (New York: Association, 1957), give insights into this important area of cultural development.

Essential for an understanding of American tragedy *in toto* though they concern only nineteenth-century writers are R. W. B. Lewis' *The American Adam: Innocence, Tragedy, and Tradition in the Nineteenth Century* (Chicago: University of Chicago Press, 1955) and Peter Thorslev's article, "Hawthorne's Determinism: An Analysis," in *Nineteenth-Century Fiction*, XIX (September, 1964), 141–57. Thorslev's set of definitions and distinctions and their literary applications can be utilized in many frames of reference other than that of Hawthorne.

The best collection of essays pertaining to American tragedy, regardless of the fact that they deal exclusively with two plays of the 1950s, is John D. Hurrell (ed.), *Two Modern American Tragedies: Reviews and Criticism of "Death of a Salesman" and "A Streetcar Named Desire"* (New York: Scribner's, 1961).

Dealing with one author only, John Longley, Jr., in *The Tragic Mask: A Study of Faulkner's Heroes* (Chapel Hill: University of North Carolina Press, 1963), nevertheless suggests ways of approaching other tragic writers. Even more particularized is Brooks Atkinson's review, " 'Streetcar' Tragedy," New York *Times*, December 14, 1947, Sec. 2, p. 2 (unaccountably not included in Hurrell). Atkinson brilliantly reminds us that tragedy is not only vision and theory, but "theater" in the broadest sense of the term, and rhetoric, and characterization.

Two tragedians, Maxwell Anderson and Arthur Miller, have written essays on the subject. Anderson's little book, *The Essence of Tragedy* (1939; reprint, New York: Russell and Russell, 1970), reveals a neoclassic approach. Miller's essay, "Tragedy and the Common Man," is obviously fundamental; it has been widely reprinted and is found in Corrigan's *Tragedy: Vision and Form* and Hurrell's *Two Modern American Tragedies*. No less important is Miller's introduction to his *Collected Plays* (New York: Viking, 1957).

Last, but only so he can be remembered best, comes John Gassner. His wisdom shines forth in two animadversions on Joseph Wood Krutch's "The Tragic Fallacy," in *The Modern Temper*, reprinted in Corrigan, Hurrell, and elsewhere. Gassner's replies are "Possibilities and Perils of Modern Tragedy," reprinted in Corrigan, *Tragedy: Vision and Form*, and "Tragedy in the Modern Theatre," in his own book *Theatre in Our Times* (New York: Crown, 1954). After the derision in which Krutch and others hold modern tragedy and after the possible suspicion that Anderson and Miller are only self-serving, Gassner sets the perspective straight by discerning both the problems and the achievements of American tragedy. Therefore, his ought to be the last word.

Index